SUPER SIMPLE QUILTS

OTHER BOOKS AVAILABLE FROM CHILTON
Robbie Fanning, Series Editor

Contemporary Quilting Series

Contemporary Quilting Techniques, by Pat Cairns
Fast Patch, by Anita Hallock
Fourteen Easy Baby Quilts, by Margaret Dittman
Machine-Quilted Jackets, Vests, and Coats,
   by Nancy Moore
*Precision Pieced Quilts Using the Foundation
   Method*, by Jane Hall and Dixie Haywood
The Quilter's Guide to Rotary Cutting,
   by Donna Poster
Quilts by the Slice, by Beckie Olson
Scrap Quilts Using Fast Patch, by Anita Hallock
Speed-Cut Quilts, by Donna Poster
Teach Yourself Machine Piecing and Quilting,
   by Debra Wagner

Creative Machine Arts Series

ABCs of Serging, by Tammy Young and Lori Bottom
The Button Lover's Book, by Marilyn Green
Claire Shaeffer's Fabric Sewing Guide
The Complete Book of Machine Embroidery,
   by Robbie and Tony Fanning
Creative Nurseries Illustrated, by Debra Terry and
   Juli Plooster
Creative Serging Illustrated, by Pati Palmer,
   Gail Brown, and Sue Green
Distinctive Serger Gifts and Crafts, by Naomi Baker
   and Tammy Young
The Fabric Lover's Scrapbook, by Margaret Dittman
Friendship Quilts by Hand and Machine,
   by Carolyn Vosburg Hall
Innovative Serging, by Gail Brown and Tammy Young
Innovative Sewing, by Gail Brown and Tammy Young
*Owner's Guide to Sewing Machines, Sergers, and
   Knitting Machines*, by Gale Grigg Hazen
Petite Pizzazz, by Barb Griffin

Putting on the Glitz, by Sandra L. Hatch and
   Ann Boyce
Sew, Serge, Press, by Jan Saunders
Sewing and Collecting Vintage Fashions,
   by Eileen MacIntosh
Simply Serge Any Fabric, by Naomi Baker and
   Tammy Young
Twenty Easy Machine-Made Rugs, by Jackie Dodson

Know Your Sewing Machine Series, by Jackie Dodson

Know Your Bernina, second edition
Know Your Brother, with Jane Warnick
Know Your Elna, with Carol Ahles
Know Your New Home, with Judi Cull and
   Vicki Lyn Hastings
Know Your Pfaff, with Audrey Griese
Know Your Sewing Machine
Know Your Singer
Know Your Viking, with Jan Saunders
Know Your White, with Jan Saunders

Know Your Serger Series, by Tammy Young and Naomi Baker

Know Your baby lock
Know Your Pfaff Hobbylock
Know Your Serger
Know Your White Superlock

Teach Yourself to Sew Better Series, by Jan Saunders

A Step-by-Step Guide to Your Bernina
A Step-by-Step Guide to Your New Home
A Step-by-Step Guide to Your Sewing Machine
A Step-by-Step Guide to Your Viking

SUPER SIMPLE
QUILTS

KATHLEEN EATON

Chilton Book Company
Radnor, Pennsylvania

To Joe, Joan, Rose and Chuck
Thank you for your loving support
and encouragement

———————————

Published in Radnor, Pennsylvania 19089, by Chilton Book Company

Designed by Anthony Jacobson

Color photography by Tim Scott
Black and white photography by Mike Boburka

Manufactured in the United States of America

Library of Congress Cataloging in Publication Data

Eaton, Kathleen.
    Super simple quilts / Kathleen Eaton.
        p.   cm. — (Contemporary quilting series)
    Includes index.
    ISBN 0-8019-8334-7 (pbk.)
    1. Quilting.   I. Title.   II. Series.
TT835.E27   1992
746.46--dc20   92-53149
                                    CIP

1 2 3 4 5 6 7 8 9 0   1 0 9 8 7 6 5 4 3 2

CONTENTS

FOREWORD

Love of quilting is moving around the globe like a giant pollinating bee. Each place it touches down, we find a harvest of new quilt lovers. At the same time, most of us have more time commitments than ever—work, family, community.

This can cause frustration: You fall in love with quilts, you want one now, yet you only have a few hours a week to sew.

Kathleen Eaton has found a clever solution. Her *Super Simple Quilts* are designed for maximum impact with minimum fuss. Because the quilts are completely machine-pieced and machine-quilted, in less than two days, you can have a gorgeous quilt on your bed.

She's done this by blowing up small portions of traditional designs, like Amish Diamond and Wild Goose Chase, much as some modern painters have done. And depending on the color and pattern combinations you choose, you can create an old-fashioned look or a contemporary one.

I like the idea that satisfaction can follow impulse in days, not months. Rather than struggle mentally with making one quilt for your bed ("will I have it on the bed in six months before my relatives come to visit?"), you can actually make a quilt for *every* bed in the same amount of time!

Robbie Fanning
Series Editor

ACKNOWLEDGMENTS

I'm grateful for the photographic talents of Michael Boburka, who assisted with black-and-white photography, and the artistic talents of Katharine Schwengel, who assisted with line drawings. Special thanks to them and to the many other people who made this book possible, especially Mom and Dad, Barb and Jim, Allison Dodge, Robbie Fanning, Tim Scott, Nancy Ziemen, Jessica, Charlie, David, Tom, Sue, and the people of the Camera Fair in Marinette, Wisconsin.

INTRODUCTION

I have always enjoyed sewing, but have learned through the years not to start a project that I know I can't complete within a reasonable amount of time. If I take on a project that is too complex, I may get bored or frustrated with it, and so it may get shelved and forgotten. Sound familiar?

These quilt patterns came about for exactly that reason. I had always wanted to make a quilt, but was intimidated by the months, or sometimes years, it took my quilting friends and neighbors to complete their projects. Even then, they weren't always satisfied with the finished results.

When I began looking for quilt patterns, I naturally tried to find something as easy as possible, since I wanted my first quilt to be a success. And, of course, it had to be beautiful, too.

Eight years later, these are still my criteria for choosing a quilt pattern. I chose the patterns in this book for their long-lasting appeal and their simplicity of construction and pattern design. The proof of the success of these quick-make patterns came when I turned my passion into a business making and selling these quilts to boutiques, catalogs, and department stores nationally.

I love the thought of choosing my own colors, or making a special gift for a special person. What a wonderful wedding or anniversary gift, or birthday present for a special child. People will think you spent weeks or months on these quilts, when, in fact, even the most difficult pattern can be completed in less than two days.

Once you have mastered a Super Simple Quilt, take it a step further by adding embellishments such as appliquéd hearts, flowers, cats, etc., to the larger, solid-colored pattern pieces. Add a name or a date in appliquéd block letters or embroidery. You can even use the 16″ pillow blocks to create a more intricately pieced quilt. Use your imagination!

A key factor in the success of these quilts is the choice and placement of fabrics. With each pattern are suggestions for choosing fabrics (see the heading "Getting Started.") Because these quilts are large, one-quilt-block patterns, it helps to define the lines and angles clearly by framing the main pattern with one solid-color fabric or a very tiny print, such as a mini-dot. In other words, no matter how beautiful the fabrics are, or how well they go together, you may lose the pattern of the quilt itself by using a combination of prints.

Instead, choose one print that you like, and build your quilt around it. The best way to know if your fabrics coordinate well is to place them side by side (without space between them) and stand back (about 10 feet, if you can).

To get an even better sense of your fabrics, you can enlarge the line drawing of your pattern on an enlarging photocopy machine, then trace it onto tracing paper. Cut out the pieces of tracing paper and use them as mini–pattern pieces to cut out pieces of fabric in the colors you'd like to use. Then paste them onto paper to see how they'd look in the finished quilt.

Remember, this is a creation of your imagination and your desire to add something beautiful to the world. No one can tell you what you like or don't like in fabric prints and colors. Just go with your instincts—if you like what you see before the quilt is even made, then the fabrics are right for you.

I've found the best combinations of fabrics for these patterns are a large print, a medium-to-small print, and a solid color fabric. If I use more than three fabrics, I try to choose one that, when placed next to the others, will stand on its own, without standing out. Sometimes a fabric that accents or brings out a lesser used color in your main print brings a spark of vitality to your whole quilt. When you are using all solid-colored fabrics, though, you want the fabrics to contrast starkly, with a range of tones from light to dark.

Remember, too, that the better the quality of the fabrics you choose, the longer the quilt will last. Even though these quilts are designed to be completed quickly, they can still give the same joy to your children and grandchildren that a more intricately pieced quilt would give. One hundred percent cotton prints are durable and machine washable, and, for the most part, they are preshrunk and colorfast. But be sure to test a swatch of fabric for possible shrinkage or fading before you start your quilt. You wouldn't want to find out the hard way, after your quilt is made, that it can't be washed. If your fabrics pass the swatch test, wash them before cutting your quilt pieces.

Decorator and designer fabrics add impact and a custom look to your quilt, but can be very expensive. They are also generally dry-clean-only. But don't let that stop you. These fabrics will last for generations, and many beautiful prints are available through discount decorating or larger fabric stores. You can even make your quilt with fabric that will match your wallpaper pattern.

Making the pattern pieces is as easy as counting squares and connecting dots. You will find instructions under "Making the Pattern" for each of the six quilts. And, once I make my patterns, I cut several quilts at once. You will notice that all my patterns are in inches, with no metric conversions. This is because it is difficult to convert inches to centimeters precisely enough for accurate piecing.

Tying your quilt is the easiest way to hold the layers together and provides a quick finish to your project. Be sure to refer to the section on tying your quilt as described for each pattern for the best placement of the ties and a description of the tying technique.

There are a number of books available on machine quilting, and if this is how you plan to finish your quilt, I suggest browsing through the local library or bookstore for books that have been written solely on this subject. Machine quilting is quite simple but takes some getting used to, especially if you have never sewn anything this bulky on your machine before.

Try taking two large pieces of scrap fabric and layering a piece of polyester fiberfill (about the same thickness as you will use for your quilt) between them. Pin or baste the layers, then practice quilting on your machine. If there is too much "drag" on the fabric, raise the presser foot a bit, if you can on your machine, or drop or cover the feed dogs, to eliminate the extra pressure on the bulk that is moving through. If you drop or cover the feed dogs, remember that you are now in control of where the quilt will go, and it will not feed through on its own. Getting used to this new method of sewing takes practice, but is well worth the effort. Once you have mastered machine quilting, you will wonder why you didn't try it sooner. Now start making those quilts and accessories for everyone on your list.

Before starting your quilt, be sure your machine is in good condition, clean and recently oiled. Change your needle, if you haven't done so recently, and check the tensions, both the upper and the bobbin, to be sure an adjustment isn't needed for this thicker work.

Here are some additional notes and tips on fabric selection for each pattern:

Amish Diamond

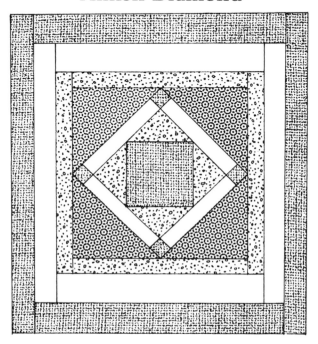

This pattern is actually a true Amish quilt pattern from the nineteenth century. The Amish people lived a very simple life, without much color or variety in their clothing, but they used vibrant color in their quilted creations. The Amish Diamond pattern is as contemporary today as it was 100 years ago. Although you will almost never find a print fabric in an authentic Amish-made quilt, that doesn't mean you can't use print fabrics in Amish designs today. See how the placement of fabrics can change the look of this quilt pattern.

This is one of many star patterns that have been created through the years, and one of the easiest. The addition of the smaller corner blocks adds to the visual impact of this quilt, though you could replace the corners with a plain square of unpieced fabric to simplify it further. Many variations on the Ohio Star have been done. One you might try is framing the center square by cutting the adjoining triangles from the same fabric.

Ohio Star

Katie's Favorite

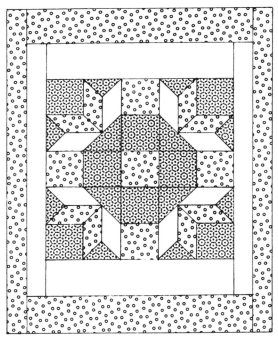

In its many variations, this pattern has also been known as Bear Paw, Turkey Tracks, Sage Bud, Sister's Choice, and Cross and Crown. Although it looks relatively intricate, it is deceiving in its simplicity. Once you have finished piecing the four goose tracks, the face is almost done. To insure success in your choice of fabrics, be sure to follow the directions under "Getting Started" for the best combinations. See how different placements of the fabric changes the finished look?

Facets

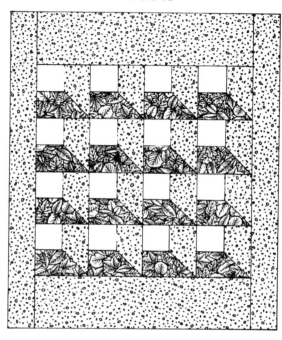

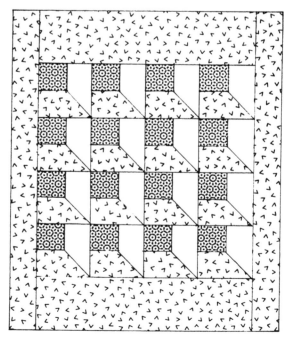

This is the simplest of the six patterns in this book—three easy pieces complete the block. I've found it is best to make the square in the quilt block the focal point. Place the darkest, lightest, or largest print here. Changing the fabric in the square changes the look of the finished quilt.

Wild Goose Chase

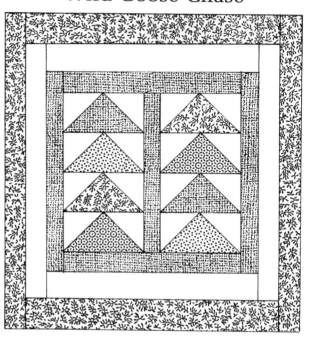

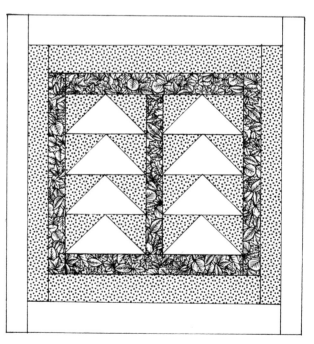

Also known as "Flying Geese," this was another popular Amish pattern, which got its name from the many directions the large triangles might take. I like to use two main fabrics in the center of this quilt and frame them with a starkly contrasting third fabric. The instructions for this quilt also include directions and fabric requirements for a multi-colored, many-fabric quilt.

Optika (Tumbling Blocks)

I have renamed this quilt "Optika" for the optical illusion that it creates. (Are they upside-down, or right-side-up?) If you are using solid-color fabrics, I recommend a very dark, a medium, and a very light color (such as black, gray, and white). This creates the "undulating" effect in the pattern.

Though this is the most difficult of the six patterns shown, you will find that once you have mastered the techniques described in the directions for piecing the rows, the rest is a snap!

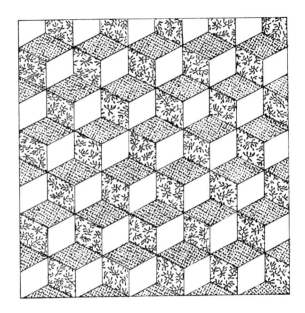

Try experimenting with fabric placement, as shown in the drawing.

I admire quiltmakers. The devotion and love that go into the beautiful works of art they create is unsurpassed. It is my hope that these quilt patterns will enable a new generation of quiltmakers to emerge, and that they will carry on a tradition that has been, for almost two centuries, a part of our national heritage.

Whether you are an expert seamstress or just beginning, these projects are right for you. And you will be pleased to know you can custom-make a quilt that will last for years, at a fraction of the cost of a store-bought comforter, in a fraction of the time you thought it would take. And you can take pride in knowing you did it yourself.

The secret of success is . . . Keep it super simple!

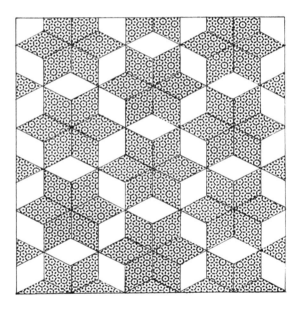

SUPER SIMPLE QUILTS #1
AMISH DIAMOND

Make a Quilt

In this section you will find all the information you need to make a twin, full, queen, or king-size quilt. Instructions for making a crib-size quilt or wall hanging begin on page 1-9.

Getting Started

This pattern actually comes from an early Amish quilt. Traditional Amish colors of dark grape, hunter green, royal blue, and black make a very pleasing combination and will give your quilt lasting appeal.

You will get the best results by using four bold, strongly contrasting colors to give optimum emphasis to the pattern. Bright red, blue, yellow, and green are a great combination, as well as softer, more pastel tones of these same colors. And teens will love a combination of white, gray, black, and red.

Materials Needed

Fabric

Yardage amounts listed below are approximate and will allow for some leftover fabric—enough to make several pillows or two pillow shams or a wall hanging or baby quilt. Yardages for backing are given in the next section.

Batting and Backing

Polyester fiberfill or wool or cotton batting large enough to complete your quilt.

A large, flat sheet or extra-wide fabric, large enough to use as a backing on your quilt. Three yards of 108″ sheeting (available at well-supplied fabric stores) will fit all sizes. Or you can use 44/45″ wide fabric as follows: *For twin and full sizes,* you need 5½ yards of 44/45″ wide fabric, cut into two pieces, each 2¾ yards long. Seam them together along the selvage (Fig. 1-1) *For queen and king sizes,* you need 8¼ yards of 44/45″ wide fabric, cut in three pieces, each 2¾ yards long, seamed together along the selvages (Fig. 1-2).

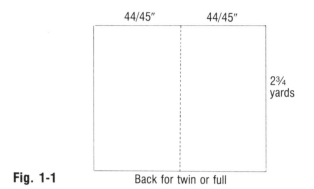

Fig. 1-1 Back for twin or full

Fig. 1-2 Back for queen or king

When laying out the backing, batting, and quilt top, center the quilt top so the seams in the back are equal distances from the sides.

Don't Forget

Thread (for piecing your quilt face, as well as for hand or machine quilting, if desired)

String, yarn, or ¹⁄₁₆″ ribbon for tying your quilt, if you prefer

Graph paper or plain paper (which you have scored with 1″ squares) for pattern making

Making the Pattern

Making the pattern is as easy as counting squares and connecting dots. The pattern guides

	Fabric 1	Fabric 2	Fabric 3	Fabric 4
Twin (90″ × 68″)	2¾ yds.	2½ yds.	1½ yds.	1⅝ yds.
Full (90″ × 76″)	2¾ yds.	2½ yds.	1½ yds.	1⅝ yds.
Queen (90″ × 90″)	2¾ yds.	2½ yds.	1½ yds.	1⅝ yds.
King (90″ × 102″)	4⅓ yds.	3¼ yds.	1½ yds.	1⅝ yds.

on pages 1-15 and 1-16 give dimensions for making your own pattern pieces for your project. You may use graph paper, gridded freezer paper, or tracing paper taped to a 1″ gridded cutting board. Graph paper is available in a variety of "squares-to-the-inch" sizes. It doesn't matter what size you choose, as long as the 1″ lines are clearly visible. If you are using smaller pieces of graph paper, carefully tape them together using clear tape, making sure the lines match up vertically and horizontally.

Start by marking a dot on the corner of one square on the grid. This represents one corner of your pattern. Using the 1″ grid on your paper, count, either straight up or down or sideways, exactly the number of inches (squares) indicated on the pattern guides on pages 1-15 and 1-16. It helps to have an extra ruler on hand to add a fraction of an inch where needed. Mark another dot when you have reached the number of squares you want, and draw a line between the dots. Continue in this manner until the pattern piece is complete.

Before drawing your angled lines, first draw the straight horizontal and vertical lines. Then just connect the ends of these lines to create the angled line to complete your pattern piece.

Do not add seam allowances! Unlike in some quilt pattern books, these patterns already include a ⅜″ seam allowance.

After you have drawn pattern pieces A through G on the grid, double-check all measurements, and carefully cut them out (Fig. 1-3).

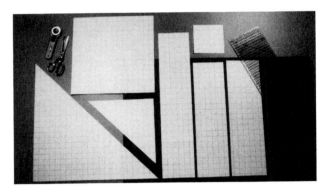

Fig. 1-3

Cutting the Fabric

Rotary cutting tools are ideal for cutting your strips and pattern pieces. Before cutting the patchwork pattern pieces, cut the side strips as follows:

Bed size	Fabric 1	Fabric 2
Twin	2 each, 11″ × 66″ 2 each, 5″ × 98″	2 each, 11″ × 56″ 2 each, 5″ × 78″
Full	2 each, 11″ × 76″ 2 each, 8″ × 98″	2 each, 11″ × 56″ 2 each, 8″ × 78″
Queen	2 each, 11″ × 78″ 2 each, 10″ × 98″	2 each, 11″ × 56″ 2 each, 10″ × 78″
King	2 each, 11″ × 84″ 2 each, 14″ × 98″	2 each, 11″ × 56″ 2 each, 14″ × 78″

Note: The center pattern of the quilt is the same for all four bed sizes. The variation in quilt size comes from the different sizes used in the side strips, which are added after the quilt center is pieced. The strip sizes shown above are generous, to allow for slight variations in seam allowances or stretch the fabric. You may trim away the excess after the strip is sewn in place.

After you have cut the long strips of fabric, cut the remaining pattern pieces. The number of pieces needed are shown on the pattern guides on pages 1-15 and 1-16.

Sewing the Main Quilt Block

Hint #1: When one or both pattern pieces are being sewn on a bias or angle-cut edge, it helps to pin the edges together to prevent pulling or stretching the fabric. Otherwise, it is not necessary to pin pieces together before sewing them. In fact, it's quicker and easier not to. Just be sure you're letting the machine do the work, and that you're not pulling, or "force-guiding," the fabric, which causes bias-cut fabrics to stretch or distort. You can also eliminate this potential problem by using a walking foot on your sewing machine.

Hint #2: Don't worry if your edges don't match perfectly when you are sewing them together. The seams are hidden inside the quilt. And the quilting stitches or ties help camouflage minor flaws. It's the total finished look that will make you proud to give or display your handiwork.

Hint #3: As you work, press all seam allowances toward the darker of the fabrics. This prevents seam allowances from being noticeable through lighter-colored fabrics.

1. After cutting out all the pieces, lay them on a flat surface (Fig. 1-4). Working from the center square, sew the pieces together using a ⅜″ seam allowance, as follows.

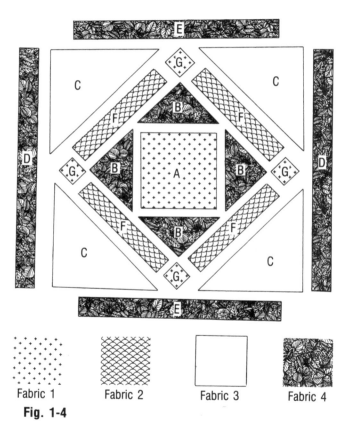

Fig. 1-4

Fabric 1   Fabric 2   Fabric 3   Fabric 4

2. Sew small triangle B to square A, centering the square so the points of the triangle are wider than the square (Fig. 1-5).

3. Sew another small triangle B to the opposite side of the square. Then sew the two remaining B triangles to the remaining sides of the square (Fig. 1-6).

Fig. 1-5

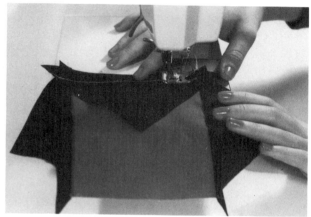

Fig. 1-6

4. Sew squares G to opposite ends of *two* F strips (Fig. 1-7).

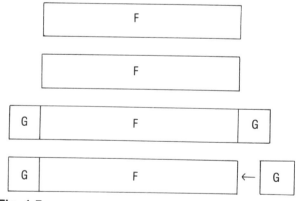

Fig. 1-7

5. Sew two F strips (without the G squares sewn on) to opposite sides of the center square (Fig. 1-8). Next sew the remaining F strips, with the G squares sewn to opposite ends, to the remaining sides, aligning the seams to create matched corners. This completes a new center square.

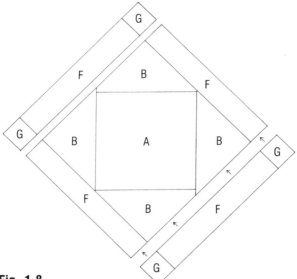

Fig. 1-8

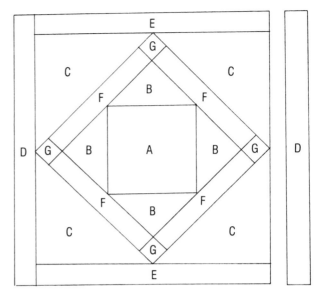

Fig. 1-10

6. Sew large triangles C to center square, as in Steps 2 and 3, complete a new center square (Fig. 1-9).

Sewing on the Side Strips

1. Sew the shorter strips of Fabric 2 to the top and bottom of your finished quilt center. (See Fig. 1-11.) Trim any excess.

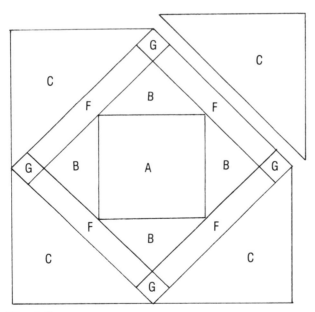

Fig. 1-9

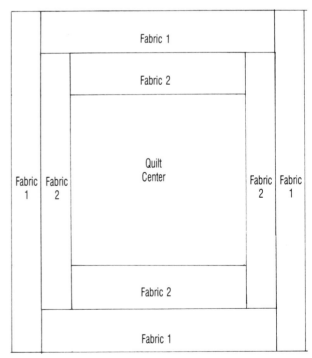

Fig. 1-11

7. Sew strips E to opposite sides of the center square. Sew strips D to the remaining sides (Fig. 1-10). You may need to trim a slight excess from these strips as they are sewn into place. Your main quilt block is now complete.

2. Sew the longer strips of Fabric 2 to the two opposite edges, including in the seam the strips that were already added (creating a large rectangle).

3. Next, sew the shorter strips of Fabric 1 to the same sides the first strips were sewn to.

4. Finally, sew the remaining (longest) strips of Fabric 1 to the last two sides of the quilt to complete the face. Press all seams toward dark.

Finishing the Quilt

1. Cut and seam the backing fabric, if necessary, to equal the size of your finished quilt top. (See directions on page 1-3.)

2. Lay the backing (sheet, sheeting, or seamed fabric) right side down on a large, clean surface.

3. Place the polyester fiberfill or other batting on top of the backing.

4. Lay the quilt top, right side up, on the fiberfill. Hand baste, or pin, using large safety pins, through all layers to hold them in place. (I prefer safety pins to straight pins because they save my hands and other body parts from pinpricks as I work.)

5. Using yarn, string, or 1/16″ ribbon, tie the layers firmly at the points shown on Fig. 1-14. Or quilt the layers by hand or machine, as desired. Instructions follow.

6. Finish the edges, using bias tape (Fig. 1-12) or other decorative trim, as desired. The edges can also be turned easily to the inside and sewn in place by machine (Fig. 1-13). You can insert piping, lace, or a ruffle at the edge with this method.

There are many ways to apply a bias taped edge, but in general, it is easiest if you sew a seam around your entire project, using a narrow seam allowance, to keep the layers from stretching or shifting *before* you apply the bias tape.

Starting in the middle of one side of your project, and using long straight pins, pin the bias tape around the entire piece, overlapping and folding under the last edge where it meets with your starting point. When you get to a corner, tuck the excess flatly and neatly inside of itself, by gently pushing it to one side with pointed scissors or a pin. It may help to open the bias tape so it is flat when you get to a corner, then pinch the excess to guide it into the fold at the corner. Hand baste or topstitch by machine over the miter.

There are a number of quilt books available with chapters devoted to finishing the edges of your quilt. Some books have been written solely on the subject. Your local library or bookstore should have a variety of books to choose from.

To Tie Your Quilt

Tying your quilt is the easiest method of holding the layers together and provides a quick finish to your quilt. I suggest basting or pinning the layers of your quilt to hold them in place before starting to tie. It is not necessary to mark the points at which you will tie your quilt. Figure 1-14 shows where the ties should be placed.

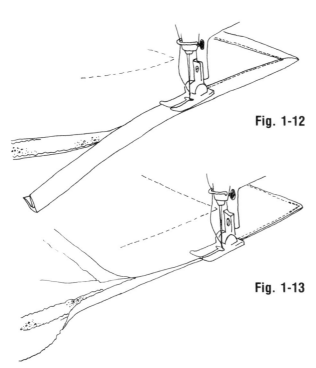

Fig. 1-12

Fig. 1-13

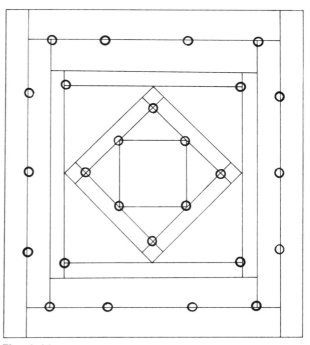

Fig. 1-14

Thread a large needle (one with a large eye, such as a tapestry needle) with yarn, $1/16''$ ribbon, or string (button or quilting thread also works well). Working from the top of the quilt, push the needle through all layers, drawing the thread through, but not all the way. Leave a $6''-8''$ tail sticking out on top. About $1/8-1/4''$ from the first stitch, draw the needle back up (from the back to the front) through all layers. Cut the thread, again leaving a tail about $6''-8''$ long. Tie these two tails tightly together, using a double or triple knot to hold the tie securely in place.

You can make a bow with the excess, or simply trim the tails to about $1''$.

To Quilt by Machine

After the layers are securely pinned or basted, roll up one-half of the quilt tightly enough to allow it to fit under the head of your sewing machine. You can safety-pin it closed or use bicycle clips to hold the roll. With larger quilts, you may need a friend to help guide the bulk through while you are quilting the center block.

Start by quilting the center area as Fig. 1-15 shows, to anchor and secure the layers. After you have stitched the quilting lines shown in Fig. 1-15, continue quilting around the center square, leaving the needle in the down position at the corners. As you go, carefully turn and reposition the quilt so the layers don't shift. It also helps to smooth the top and bottom toward you occasionally, with one hand above and one hand below, palms pressed gently together, and fingers spread.

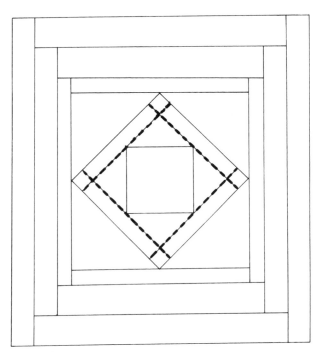

Fig. 1-15

Continue quilting by machine, following the outline of the pattern by sewing along all the seam lines of the pieced quilt top. Be sure to back-tack the beginning and ending of each quilting seam. I like to use thread that matches one of the lighter fabrics. When quilting along a seam that joins a solid color to a print fabric, try to keep your quilting stitches on the printed fabric, just to the side of the seam.

Today's polyester fiberfills don't clump or shift as much as natural battings made of wool or cotton, because of the resins that hold the polyester fibers together. The stitching lines suggested here are adequate to hold polyester fiberfill in place, but you may wish to add some extra quilting lines or ties if using pure wool or cotton batting.

Alternate Method of Finishing

1. Another method of finishing your quilt is to sew the face to the backing, right sides together, leaving the top edge open. Because these seams are so long, it helps to pin the edges together before sewing, to hold them in place. Be sure the back is cut to the exact size of the face before sewing them together.

2. Before turning right side out, lay your top and backing, which have been sewn together on three sides, right side down on a large, clean, flat surface. If you don't have a large enough floor space, lay it on as large a table as you can, with the open, unseamed end hanging over the edge of the table, and the bottom half of the quilt lying flat on the table. Place the polyester fiberfill on top and trim it to the exact size of the quilt.

3. Starting at the end opposite the opening, roll the entire quilt, like a sleeping bag, or jelly roll, until you have a long "tube" of fabric and batting (Fig. 1-16).

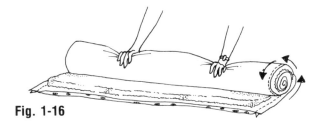

Fig. 1-16

4. Carefully reach inside the layers of fabric (between the face and backing), and slowly pull the tube inside-out, through the opening (Fig. 1-17).

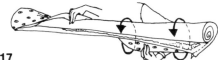

Fig. 1-17

5. Slowly unwrap the quilt (Fig. 1-18), which will open, filled with fiberfill, and with three of the edges finished. (Practice with a sock. First, roll the sock, starting at the toe, and pull the cuff back over the roll. Slowly unroll it from the inside out, reaching inside the sock, between the layers, and pulling gently on the roll.)

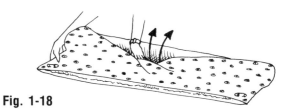

Fig. 1-18

6. Lay the quilt on a large, flat surface, and pin or baste through all layers. Hand or machine quilt, or tie it, as described above.

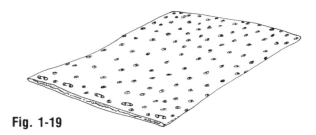

Fig. 1-19

7. Turn the remaining edges to the inside, pin to hold (Fig. 1-19), and machine stitch to close.

Make a Crib Quilt (42″ × 52″)

Materials Needed

Fabric

Fabric 1, 1¾ yards
Fabric 2, ⅓ yard
Fabric 3 and 4, ½ yard each

Batting and Backing

Polyester fiberfill: 44″ × 54″
Backing fabric: 1¾ yards of 44/45″ wide fabric

Don't Forget

Thread (for piecing your quilt face, as well as for hand or machine quilting, if desired)
String, yarn, or 1/16″ ribbon for tying your quilt, if you prefer
Graph paper or plain paper (which you have scored with 1″ squares) for pattern making

1. Make your pattern pieces A through G in the dimensions given on the pattern guides on pages 1-15 and 1-16. Refer to "Getting Started" and "Making the Pattern" in the instructions for the large quilts. (This pattern is simply a miniature version of the main quilt block of the large quilt, minus one of the side strips.)

2. Before cutting pieces A through G out of your fabric, cut the side strips out of Fabric 1: two pieces 8″ × 39″ and two pieces 4″ × 54″.

3. Now cut out fabric pieces A through G.

4. Refer to "Sewing the Main Quilt Block," "Sewing on the Side Strips," and "Finishing the Quilt" in the instructions for the large quilts to complete the crib quilt. (You will be adding only one set of side strips.) The "Alternate Method of Finishing" (p. 1-8) is particularly nice when used on the crib quilt project.

Make a Wall Hanging (36″ square)

Materials Needed

Fabric

Fabric 1, ⅓ yard
Fabric 2, ⅓ yard

Fabrics 3 and 4, ½ yard each

Batting and Backing

Polyester fiberfill: 38″ square
Backing fabric: 1¼ yards, cut to fit face of wall hanging

Don't Forget

Thread (for piecing your quilt face, as well as for hand or machine quilting, if desired)

String, yarn, or 1/16″ ribbon for tying your quilt, if you prefer

Graph paper or plain paper (which you have scored with 1″ squares) for pattern making

1. Make your pattern pieces A through G in the dimensions given on the pattern guides on pages 1-15 and 1-16. Refer to "Getting Started" and "Making the Pattern" in the instructions for the large quilts. (This pattern is simply a miniature version of the main quilt block of the large quilt; no additional side strips are used for the wall hanging.)

2. Cut out all fabric pieces.

3. Refer to "Sewing the Main Quilt Block" and "Finishing the Quilt" in the instructions for the large quilts to complete the wall hanging. (The wall hanging has no added side strips.) The "Alternate Method of Finishing" (p. 1-8) is particularly nice when used on the wall hanging project.

You will probably want to make loops of fabric to sew to the top of the wall hanging or just behind the upper edge (hidden) to allow for a dowel rod to hang it.

To Make the Loops

For **hidden loops**, cut three pieces of fabric 1½″ × 4″. Fold the long edges inward to meet at the center, then fold the whole strip in half lengthwise. Using a straight stitch, sew through all layers along the "open" edge to make a small "ribbon" of fabric. Attach one in the middle of the upper edge of the wall hanging, and the remaining two at either side on the upper edge. Tack these to the

wall hanging through all layers using your sewing machine, or hand sew them in place.

For **decorative loops** (Fig. 1-20), cut three pieces of matching fabric 3″ × 5″. Fold these in half, right sides together, to create 1½″ × 5″ pieces. Using a ⅜″ seam allowance, sew a straight line down the 5″ raw edge. Turn these tubes right side out and press so the seam is centered on one side. Fold these in half widthwise to hide the seam. Attach to the top of your wall hanging by machine, spacing the loops evenly.

For **bow loops**, cut three pieces of wide ribbon, each 24″ long. Fold these in half and tack them to the top edge of your wall hanging by hand or machine, evenly spaced. Tie these loosely around a decorative pole or dowel rod.

The wall hanging is a perfect size for use as a table topper, lap quilt, or sofa throw.

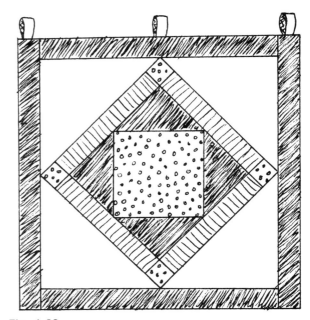

Fig. 1-20

Make a 16″ Throw Pillow

Fabric Requirements

Face: Use leftover scrap from large quilt or ⅛ yard of each of the four fabrics

Back: ½ yard of a matching fabric or a coordinating solid

Ruffle or cord: ⅝ yard of a matching fabric to make your own matching ruffle or bias cording. Or purchase 2 yards of prepackaged bias cording or ruffle.

1. Make pillow pattern pieces A through G in the dimensions given in the pattern guides on pages 1-15 and 1-16. See "Getting Started" and "Making the Pattern" in the instructions for the large quilt. Cut all fabric pieces.

2. Starting with the center square, and using a ⅜″ seam allowance, sew all pieces to complete the block according to Figs. 1-4 through 1-10. Press all seams toward darker fabrics.

3. You may quilt the pillow face before constructing the pillow. If so, layer it with a backing and fiberfill, cut to the same size as the face, then hand or machine quilt along the seams. It is not necessary to quilt the pillow; this is a matter of preference.

4. See the instructions for making ruffling and bias cording, page 1-12 With raw edges together, sew bias cording or a ruffle around the entire pillow face with a ⅜″ seam allowance. The raw edges of the cording match the raw edges of the pillow face (Fig. 1-21). You will need about 2 yards of bias cording or finished ruffling to go around the pillow. For a knife-edge pillow, with no extra trim, you can eliminate this step.

Fig. 1-21

5. Cut two pieces of backing fabric, 10″ × 17″. Finish one 17″ edge on each of these two pieces with a double-folded ¼″ hem, machine stitched.

6. Lay the pillow right side up, with ruffle or cording toward the center. Place the backing right side down on the pillow, overlapping the finished edges evenly in the center. Pin around the edges (Fig. 1-22).

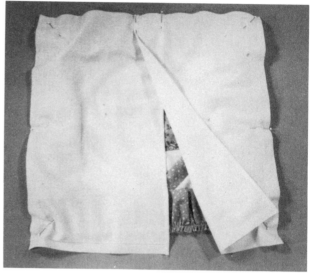

Fig. 1-22

7. Sew around the entire pillow, following the seam used to sew the cording or ruffle in place, or using a ⅜″ seam allowance. Turn inside out through the overlapped backing. Trim away any excess around the seams before turning.

8. Insert a 15″ or 16″ pillow form.

Make Your Own 15″–16″ Pillow Form

1. Save your scrap fiberfill.

2. Cut two 18″ squares of any white or ivory fabric.

3. Sew these together on three sides, using a ½″ seam allowance. Turn right side out.

4. Cut two 17″ squares of leftover fiberfill, and carefully slide them into the pillow cover. Continue to stuff smaller bits of fiberfill between the squares, until the pillow is plump, but not too hard.

5. To finish, whipstitch the opening by hand. I call this a 15″–16″ finished size because the finished size will vary according to the plumpness of the pillow.

Make a Removable Chair Pad Cover

Note: An additional ⅓ yard of one of the fabrics is required for each chair pad.

1. Complete the 16″ pillow cover as explained above in "Make a 16″ Throw Pillow."

2. Cut two strips of fabric, 44″ × 5″. With a roll-hem attachment for your sewing machine, or a narrow double fold, hem around all sides of both strips. Fold each in half, matching the two short ends to create two tie ends, and pinch or pleat at

the fold to gather. At what will be the back two corners, machine stitch the ties to the pillow cover, on the underside of the finished pillow, under the ruffle (Fig. 1-23).

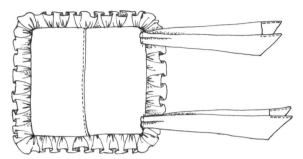

Fig. 1-23

3. To make a removable chair pad insert, purchase or make a 15″–16″ pillow form. With a long needle and double heavy-duty thread, run the thread through the center of the pillow form, leaving a "tail" of thread about 6″ long. Bring the needle back through about ½″ from the first stitch, and tie the ends of the thread, pulling tightly to form a "tuft" in the center.

Two matching chair pads make a lovely rocker set. (Fig. 1-24).

Fig. 1-24

How to Make Matching Ruffling and Bias Cording for Pillows, Shams, and Chair Pads

Ruffling

You will need about ⅝″ yard of extra fabric for ruffles around pillows and chair pads. You will need about ⅞ yard for pillow shams.

1. From the width of the fabric (44/45″) cut three 7″ strips (four strips for pillow shams), and sew them together on the short ends to make a long circle of fabric. Press the seam allowances open.

2. Fold the circle in half lengthwise so the raw edges meet and right sides face out. Press.

3. With a wide basting stitch, sew about ¼″ from the raw edge (Fig. 1-25).

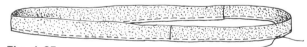

Fig. 1-25

4. Divide the circle equally into quarters, identifying the quarter marks with a straight pin. Pin the circle to the center of each straight edge on all four sides of your project, using the pins that mark the quarters to hold the ruffle in place.

5. Pull the basting stitch until the circle gathers evenly into a ruffle equal to the size of the project that you are working on. Use straight pins to hold the ruffle in place around the outer edge of the project as you gather it to fit (Fig. 1-26).

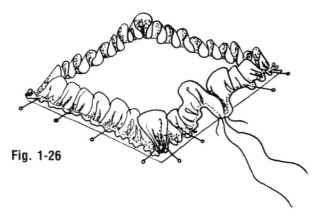

Fig. 1-26

Bias Cording

You will need ⅝ yard of matching fabric to make your own bias cording.

1. Cut 1½"-wide strips of fabric on the bias of the fabric. The strip of bias-cut fabric should be several inches longer than the measurement around the edge of the project you wish to trim. You may have to seam your pieces to arrive at the proper length.

2. Using purchased cording, wrap the bias strip around the cording so that wrong sides and raw edges meet. Using a zipper foot, stitch close to the cord, but not too snug, through both layers of fabric (Fig. 1-27).

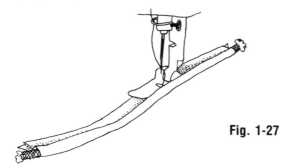

Fig. 1-27

3. The simplest application of the finished bias tape is to begin sewing it on one straight edge in the center of that side, keeping the raw edges of the bias tape and your project even, but with the starting end angled off the edge. Sew around the entire project, clipping the seam allowance of the bias tape at the corners. When you reach your starting point, overlap the bias tape, sewing over the angled end, and carefully angle the final end to sew it off the edge (Fig. 1-28). Clip it to trim.

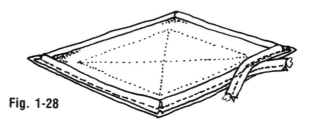

Fig. 1-28

You may also apply bias tape by starting in the middle of one side, but start your seam about 2" from the end of the bias tape. Sew all around as described above, but when you get to where you started, open the seam on the 2" tail of the bias tape and pull back the fabric to show the cord. Clip off the 2" of cord, and fold the fabric that is left in half, to create a 1" tail (fold the fabric to the inside, so that only the face side shows). Cut the other end of the bias tape so it ends exactly where the first cord now starts. Wrap the folded bias tape fabric around this raw edge, and finish your seam.

Make a Placemat

Fabric Requirements

Face: Use leftover scrap from quilt or ⅛ yard of each of the four fabrics

Back: ½ yard of fabric will allow enough for two placemats

1. Make your pattern pieces A through G in the dimensions given on the pattern guides on pages 1-15 and 1-16. See "Getting Started" and "Making the Pattern" in the instructions for the large quilts. Cut out all fabric pieces.

2. Starting with the center square, and using a ⅜" seam allowance, sew all pieces to complete the block according to Figs. 1-4 through 1-10. Press all seams toward darker fabric.

3. Cut two strips of fabric, 2½" × 17", and sew them to opposite sides of the finished quilt block, trimming away any excess. Press all seams. This makes the placemat rectangular.

4. Cut a rectangle of backing fabric 17" × 20". Center this, right sides together, on the finished quilt block. Trim excess fabric from the quilt block to equal the size of the backing. Sew together with a ³⁄₈″ seam allowance all around, except for a 4″ opening centered on one of the seams. Clip the corners and turn inside out through the opening. Hand or machine stitch the opening and press all around.

5. To minimize raveling or fraying of the seams on the inside when these are washed, you may wish to "quilt" along the seam lines, even though these do not have fiberfill. (You may add fiberfill, if you wish.)

Make a Standard Pillow Sham

Fabric Requirements

Face: Use leftover scrap from quilt, or ¼ yard of Fabrics 1 and 2 and ⅛ yard of Fabrics 3 and 4

Back: ⅔ yard

Ruffle: ⅞ yard

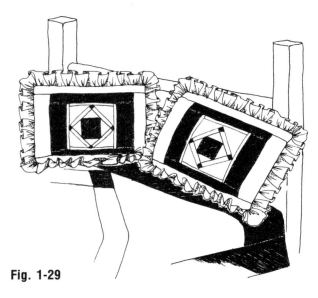

Fig. 1-29

1. Make your pattern pieces A through G in the dimensions given on the pattern guides on pages 1-15 and 1-16. See "Getting Started" and "Making the Pattern" in the instructions for the large quilts. Cut out all fabric pieces.

2. Starting with the center square and using a ³⁄₈″ seam allowance, sew all pieces to complete the block according to Figs. 1-4 through 1-10. Press all seams toward dark.

3. Cut two strips of Fabric 2, 3½″ × 17″, and two strips 2″ × 23″.

4. Cut two strips of Fabric 1, 3½″ × 21″, and two strips 2″ × 29″.

5. Add the 3½″ × 17″ strips of Fabric 2 to opposite sides of the quilt block, trimming away any excess. Add the 2″ × 23″ strips of the same fabric, in the same manner, to the remaining edges.

6. Add the 3½″ × 21″ strips of Fabric 1 to the first sides (as in Step 5), and add the remaining strips to the last two sides.

7. You may wish to first quilt the sham face by layering it with a backing and fiberfill cut to the same size as the face, then hand or machine quilt along the seams. This is not necessary. It's a matter of preference.

8. See the instructions for making ruffling and bias cording, page 1-12. With raw edges together, sew bias cording and/or a ruffle around the entire sham face with a ³⁄₈″ seam allowance. You will need about 3 yards of bias cording or finished ruffling to go around the pillow sham. (This is sewn to the face side of the pillow sham.)

9. Cut two pieces of a backing fabric, 16″ × 24″, finishing one 24″ edge on each piece with a narrow double-folded ¼″ hem, machine stitched.

10. Lay the pillow sham right side up, with ruffle pressed toward the center (Fig. 1-21). Place the backing, right side down, on the sham, overlapping the finished edges evenly in the center. Pin around the edges (see Fig. 1-22). Flip it over.

11. Sew around the entire pillow sham, following the seam used to sew the ruffling and/or cording in place. Turn inside out through the overlapped backing. Trim away any excess around the seams before turning right side out.

Amish Diamond Pattern Guides

Dimensions include ⅜″ seam allowance.

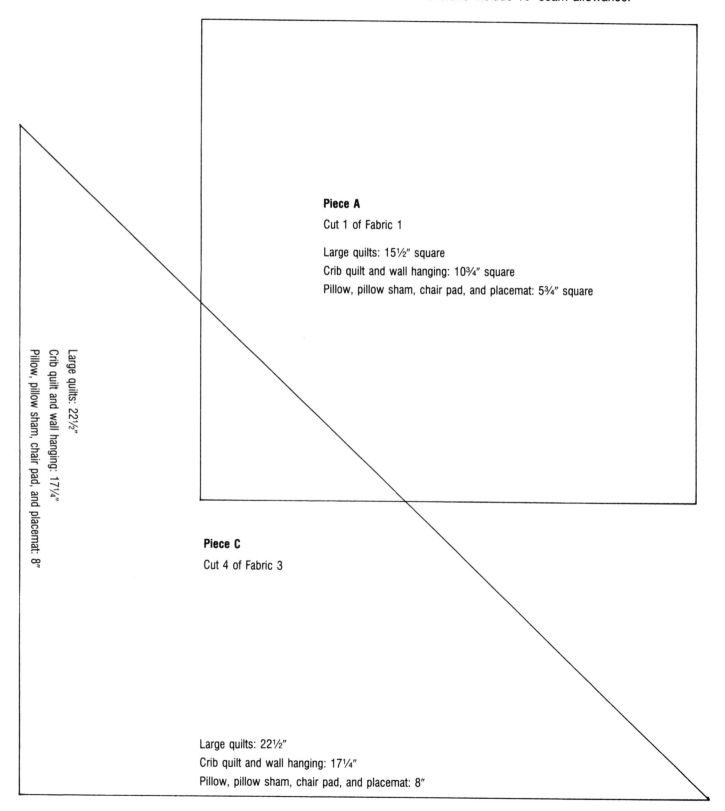

Piece A

Cut 1 of Fabric 1

Large quilts: 15½″ square
Crib quilt and wall hanging: 10¾″ square
Pillow, pillow sham, chair pad, and placemat: 5¾″ square

Piece C

Cut 4 of Fabric 3

Large quilts: 22½″
Crib quilt and wall hanging: 17¼″
Pillow, pillow sham, chair pad, and placemat: 8″

Large quilts: 22½″
Crib quilt and wall hanging: 17¼″
Pillow, pillow sham, chair pad, and placemat: 8″

Note: Instructions for making your templates in the correct dimensions can be found under "Making the Pattern".

Amish Diamond Pattern Guides

Dimensions include ⅜″ seam allowance.

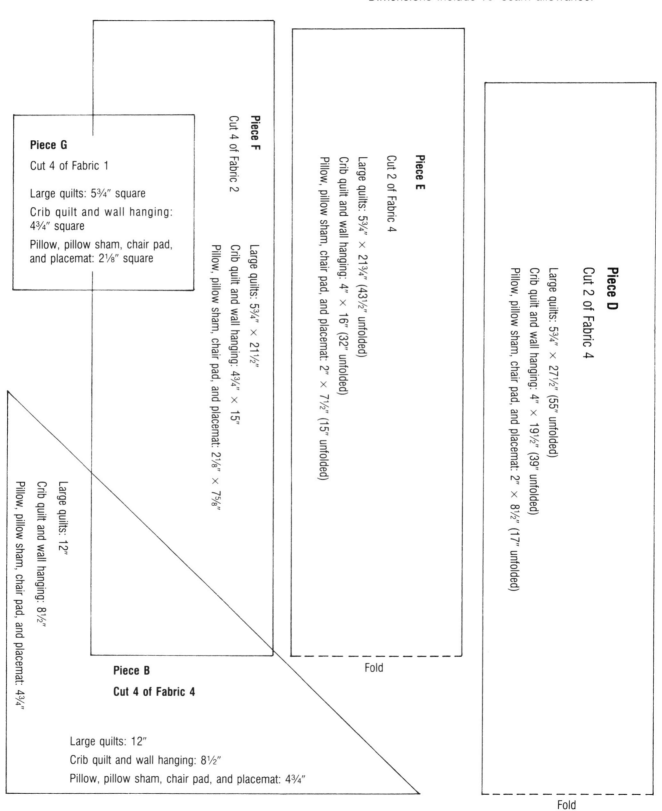

Piece G

Cut 4 of Fabric 1

Large quilts: 5¾″ square

Crib quilt and wall hanging: 4¾″ square

Pillow, pillow sham, chair pad, and placemat: 2⅛″ square

Piece F

Cut 4 of Fabric 2

Large quilts: 5¾″ × 21½″

Crib quilt and wall hanging: 4¾″ × 15″

Pillow, pillow sham, chair pad, and placemat: 2⅛″ × 7⅝″

Piece E

Cut 2 of Fabric 4

Large quilts: 5¾″ × 21¾″ (43½″ unfolded)

Crib quilt and wall hanging: 4″ × 16″ (32″ unfolded)

Pillow, pillow sham, chair pad, and placemat: 2″ × 7½″ (15″ unfolded)

Piece D

Cut 2 of Fabric 4

Large quilts: 5¾″ × 27½″ (55″ unfolded)

Crib quilt and wall hanging: 4″ × 19½″ (39″ unfolded)

Pillow, pillow sham, chair pad, and placemat: 2″ × 8½″ (17″ unfolded)

Large quilts: 12″

Crib quilt and wall hanging: 8½″

Pillow, pillow sham, chair pad, and placemat: 4¾″

Piece B

Cut 4 of Fabric 4

Large quilts: 12″

Crib quilt and wall hanging: 8½″

Pillow, pillow sham, chair pad, and placemat: 4¾″

Fold

Fold

SUPER SIMPLE QUILTS #2
OHIO STAR

20544

A. FEIBUSCH CORPORATION

27 ALLEN STREET • NEW YORK, NY 10002
TEL: 888-947-7872 • 212-226-3964 • FAX 212-226-5844
WWW.ZIPPERSTOP.COM   E-MAIL: AFEIBUSCH@PRODIGY.NET

ZIPPERS

THREADS • GARMENT SUPPLIES

DATE _3/14/05_

NAME _Jennifer Yantachka,_

ADDRESS _____

CITY _____ STATE _____ ZIP CODE _____

QUAN.	DESCRIPTION	PRICE	AMOUNT
	814026 0377		
	paid		
	Paypal		
	SHIPPING & HANDLING		
	SALES TAX		
	TOTAL		

ALL CLAIMS MUST BE MADE
WITHIN 7 DAYS.

Make a Quilt

In this section you will find all the information you need to make a twin, full, queen, or king-size quilt. Instructions for making a crib-size quilt or wall hanging begin on page 2-9.

Getting Started

The Ohio Star bed-size quilt features one large star in the middle, framed by four stars in the corners. You will need three fabrics for this project. You will get excellent results by using two contrasting prints with a light-colored solid. Or try a print with one dark and one light solid.

Materials Needed

Fabric

Yardage amounts listed below are approximate and will allow for some leftover fabric—enough to make several pillows or two pillow shams or a wall hanging or baby quilt. Yardages for backing fabric are listed in the following section.

Batting and Backing

Polyester fiberfill or wool or cotton batting large enough to complete your quilt.

A large, flat sheet or extra-wide fabric, large enough to use as a backing on your quilt. Three yards of 108″ sheeting (available at well-supplied fabric stores) will fit all sizes. Or, you can use 44/45″ wide fabric as follows: For twin and full sizes, you need 5½ yards of 44/45″ wide fabric, cut into two pieces, each 2¾ yards long. Seam them together along the selvages (Fig. 2-1). For queen and king sizes, you need 8¼ yards of 44/45″ wide fabric, cut in three pieces, each 2¾ yards, seamed together along the selvages (Fig. 2-2).

When laying out the backing, batting, and quilt top, center the quilt top so the seams in the back are equal distances from the sides.

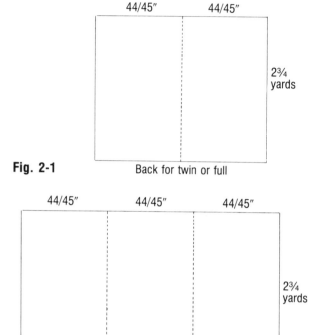

Fig. 2-1 Back for twin or full

Fig. 2-2 Back for queen or king

Don't Forget

Thread (for piecing your quilt face, as well as for hand or machine quilting, if desired)

String, yarn, or 1/16″ ribbon for tying your quilt, if you prefer

Graph paper or plain paper (which you have scored with 1″ squares) for pattern making

Making the Pattern

Making the pattern is as easy as counting squares and connecting dots. The pattern guides on pages 2-15 and 2-16 give dimensions for making your own pattern pieces. You may use graph

	Fabric 1	Fabric 2	Fabric 3
Twin (90″ × 68″)	3½ yards	3 yards	2 yards
Full (90″ × 76″)	4 yards	3 yards	2 yards
Queen (90″ × 90″)	4 yards	3 yards	2 yards
King (90″ × 102″)	5 yards	4 yards	2 yards

paper, gridded freezer paper, or tracing paper taped to a 1″ gridded cutting board. Graph paper is available in a variety of "squares-to-the-inch" sizes. It doesn't matter what size you choose, as long as the 1″ lines are clearly visible. If you are using smaller pieces of graph paper, carefully tape them together using clear tape, making sure the lines match up vertically and horizontally.

Start by marking a dot on the corner of one square on the grid. This represents one corner of your pattern. Using the 1″ grid on your paper, count, either straight up or down or sideways, exactly the number of inches (squares) shown on the pattern guides on pages 2-15 and 2-16. It helps to have an extra ruler on hand to add a fraction of an inch where needed. Mark another dot when you have reached the number of squares you want, and draw a line between the dots. Continue in this manner until the pattern piece is complete.

Before drawing your angled lines, first draw the straight horizontal and vertical lines. Then just connect the ends of these lines to create the angled line to complete your pattern piece.

Do not add seam allowances! Unlike in some quilt pattern books, these patterns already include a ⅜″ seam allowance.

After you have drawn your pattern pieces on the grid, double-check all measurements, and carefully cut them out.

Cutting the Fabric

Rotary cutting tools are ideal for cutting your strips and pattern pieces. Before cutting the patch-work pattern pieces, cut the side strips as follows:

Bed size	Fabric 1	Fabric 2
Twin	2 each, 11″ × 68″ 2 each, 5″ × 98″	2 each, 11″ × 56″ 2 each, 5″ × 78″
Full	2 each, 11″ × 76″ 2 each, 8″ × 98″	2 each, 11″ × 56″ 2 each, 8″ × 78″
Queen	2 each, 11″ × 78″ 2 each, 10″ × 98″	2 each, 11″ × 56″ 2 each, 10″ × 78″
King	2 each, 11″ × 84″ 2 each, 14″ × 98″	2 each, 11″ × 56″ 2 each, 14″ × 78″

Note: The center pattern of the quilt is the same for all four bed sizes. The variation in quilt size comes from the different sizes used in the side strips, which are added after the quilt center is pieced. The strip sizes shown above are generous to allow for slight variations in seam allowances or stretch of the fabric. You may trim away the excess after the strip is sewn in place.

After you have cut the long strips of fabric, cut the remaining pattern pieces. The number of pieces needed are shown on the pattern guides at the end of this project.

Sewing the Main Quilt Block

Hint #1: When one or both pattern pieces are being sewn on a bias or angle-cut edge, it helps to pin the edges together to prevent pulling or stretching the fabric. Otherwise, it is not necessary to pin pieces together before sewing them. In fact, it's quicker and easier not to. Just be sure you're

letting the machine do the work, and that you're not pulling, or "force-guiding," the fabric, which causes bias-cut fabrics to stretch or distort. You can also eliminate this potential problem by using a walking foot on your sewing machine.

Hint #2: Don't worry if your edges don't match perfectly when you are sewing them together. The seams are hidden inside the quilt. And the quilting stitches or ties help camouflage minor flaws. It's the total finished look that will make you proud to give or display your handiwork.

Hint #3: As you work, press all seam allowances toward the darker of the fabrics. This prevents seam allowances from being noticeable through lighter-colored fabrics.

1. After cutting out all pattern pieces, lay out the *large* triangles (Fabrics 1 and 3) as shown in Fig. 2-3. Using a ⅜″ seam allowance, sew the pieces together as shown in Figs. 2-4 through 2-6 to create

Amish Diamond wall hanging.

Ohio Star chair pad and placemat.

Katie's Favorite quilt, pillow sham, and pillow.

Facets placemats.

Wild Goose Chase quilt, pillow sham, and pillow.

Optika wall hanging and pillow.

Wild Goose Chase crib quilt.

Amish Diamond pillows.

Ohio Star.

four large squares. When seams intersect, I prefer to press the intersecting seam allowances toward the darker of the fabrics. Clip the final seam allowance at the center of the finished square, and press these seam allowances toward the darker fabric. This helps keep seam allowances from showing through lighter-colored fabrics. Remember to back-tack at the beginning and end of all seams.

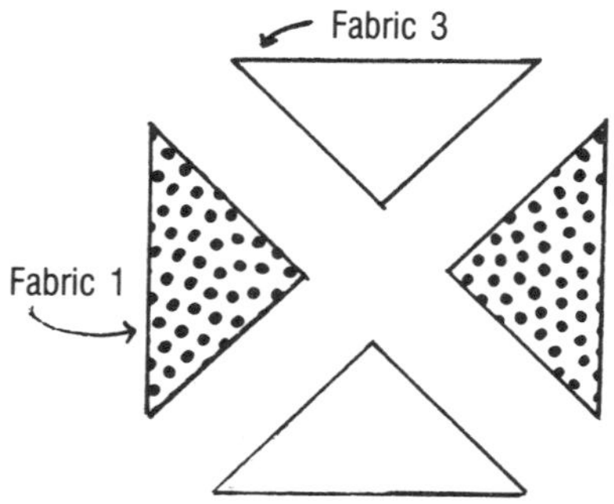

Fig. 2-3

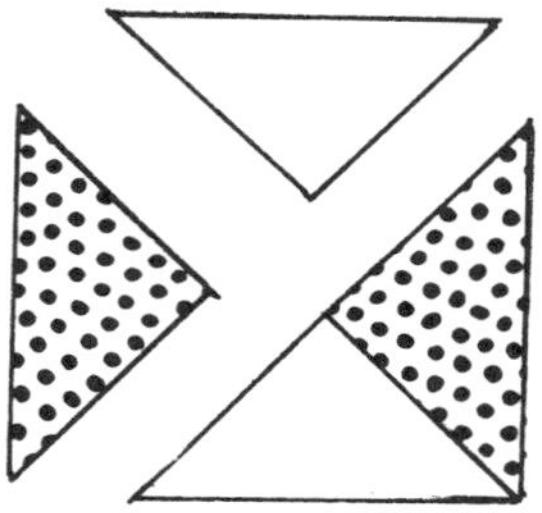

Fig. 2-4

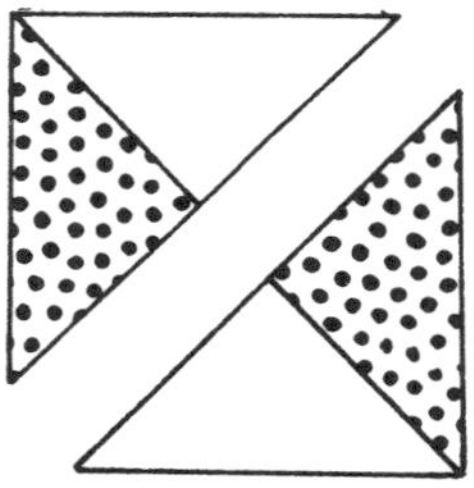

Fig. 2-5

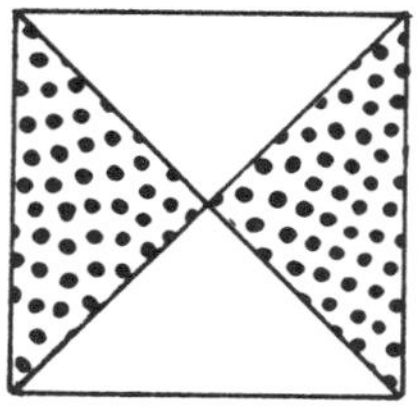

Fig. 2-6

2. Now lay out the *small* triangles (Fabrics 1 and 3) in the same manner as the large ones (see Step 1 and Fig. 2-3). With ⅜″ seam allowances, piece these triangles into 16 small squares (see Figs. 2-4 through 2-6).

3. Arrange your *small* pieced blocks and *small* solid blocks (Fabrics 2 and 3) as shown in Fig. 2-7. Sew them together into rows, then sew the three rows together to create a square (Fig. 2-8). Continue until you have completed four "Ohio Stars."

Fig. 2-7

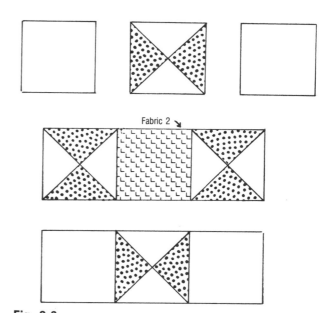

Fig. 2-8

4. Now arrange the four pieced Ohio Star blocks with the fabric squares you pieced in Step 1 and your large solid square (Fabric 2) as shown in Fig. 2-9. Sew these together as in Step 3, first creating three long strips, then sewing the strips together to create the finished center of the quilt. Press all seams.

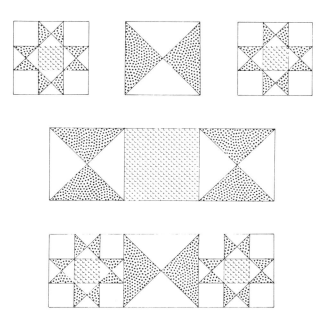

Fig. 2-9

Sewing on the Side Strips

1. After you decide which two sides of the finished quilt center you prefer to be the top and bottom, sew the shorter strips of Fabric 2 to these edges. Trim any excess.

2. Sew the longer strips of Fabric 2 to the two remaining edges, including in the seam the strips that were already added

3. Next, sew the shorter strips of Fabric 1 to the same sides the first strips were sewn to. Trim excess.

4. Finally, sew the remaining longest strips of Fabric 1 to the last two sides of the quilt to complete the face (Fig. 2-10). Press all seams toward dark.

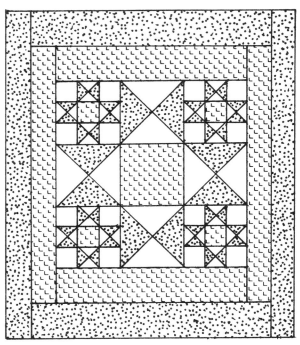

Fig. 2-10

Finishing the Quilt

1. Cut and seam the backing fabric, if necessary, to equal the size of your finished quilt top (see Figs. 2-1, 2-2).

2. Lay the backing (sheet, sheeting, or seamed fabric) right side down on a large, clean surface.

3. Place the polyester fiberfill or other batting on top of the backing.

4. Lay the quilt top right side up on the fiberfill. Hand baste, or pin using large safety pins, through all layers to hold them in place (Fig. 2-11). (I prefer

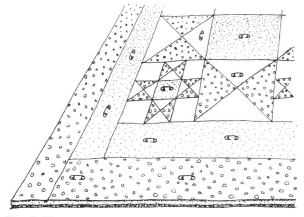

Fig. 2-11

safety pins to straight pins because they save my hands and other body parts from pinpricks as I work.)

5. Using yarn, string, or ¹⁄₁₆″ ribbon, tie the layers firmly, or quilt the layers by hand or machine, as desired. Instructions follow.

6. Finish the edges, using bias tape or other decorative trim, as desired (Fig. 2-12). The edges can also be turned easily to the inside and sewn in place by machine (Fig. 2-13). You can insert piping, lace, or a ruffle at the edge with this method.

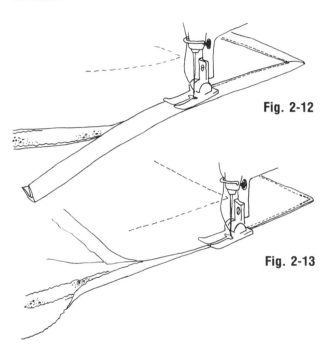

Fig. 2-12

Fig. 2-13

There are many ways to apply a bias taped edge, but, in general, it is easiest if you sew a seam around your entire project, using a narrow seam allowance, to keep the layers from stretching or shifting *before* you apply the bias tape.

Starting in the middle of one side of your project, and using long straight pins, pin the bias tape around the entire piece, overlapping and folding under the last edge where it meets with your starting point. When you get to a corner, tuck the excess flatly and neatly inside of itself, by gently pushing it to one side with a pointed scissor or pin. It may help to open the bias tape so it is flat when you get to a corner, then pinch the excess to guide it into the fold at the corner. Hand baste or topstitch by machine over the miter.

There are a number of quilt books available with chapters devoted to finishing the edges of your quilt. Some books have been written solely on the subject. Your local library or bookstore should have a variety of books to choose from.

To Tie Your Quilt

Tying your quilt is the easiest method of holding the layers together and provides a quick finish to your quilt. Baste or pin the layers of your quilt to hold them in place before starting to tie. It is not necessary to mark the points at which you will tie your quilt. Figure 2-14 shows where the ties should be placed.

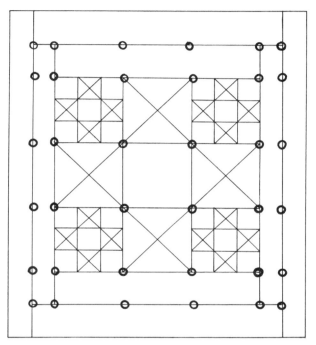

Fig. 2-14

Thread a large needle (one with a large eye, such as a tapestry needle) with yarn, ¹⁄₁₆″ ribbon, or string (button or quilting thread also works well). Working from the top of the quilt, push the needle through all layers, drawing the thread through, but not all the way. Leave a 6″–8″ tail sticking out on top. About ¹⁄₈″–¹⁄₄″ from the first stitch, draw the needle back up (from the back to the front) through all layers. Cut the thread, again leaving a tail about 6″–8″ long. Tie these two tails tightly together, using a double or triple knot to hold the tie securely in place.

You can make a bow with the excess, or simply trim the tails to about 1″.

To Quilt by Machine

After the layers are securely pinned or basted, roll up one-half of the quilt tightly enough to allow it to fit under the head of your sewing machine.

You can safety-pin it closed or use bicycle clips to hold the roll. With larger quilts, you may need a friend to help guide the bulk through while you are quilting the center block (Fig. 2-15).

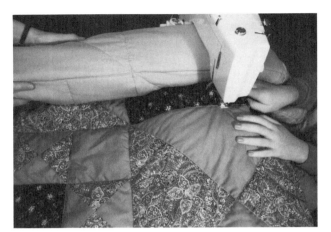

Fig. 2-15

Starting with the seams shown in Fig. 2-16, stitch "anchoring" quilt lines to hold all layers in place. This stitching will secure all layers of fabric and help keep the remainder of the quilt from shifting. It also helps to smooth the top and bottom toward you occasionally, with one hand above and one hand below, palms pressed gently together, and fingers spread.

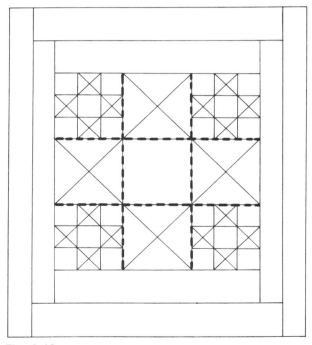

Fig. 2-16

After you have stitched the lines shown in Fig. 2-16, continue quilting by machine, following the outline of the pattern by sewing along the seam lines of the pieced quilt top. Be sure to back-tack the beginning and ending of each quilting seam. I like to use thread that matches one of the lighter fabrics. When quilting along a seam that joins a solid color to a print fabric, try to keep your quilting stitches on the printed fabric, to the side of the seam.

Today's polyester fiberfills don't clump or shift as much as natural battings made of wool or cotton, because of the resins that hold the polyester fibers together. The stitching lines suggested here are adequate to hold polyester fiberfill in place, but you may wish to add some extra quilting lines or ties if you use pure wool or cotton batting.

Alternate Method of Finishing

1. Another method of finishing your quilt is to sew the face to the backing, right sides together, leaving the top edge open. Because these seams are so long, it helps to pin the edges together before sewing, to hold them in place. Be sure the backing is cut to the exact size of the face before sewing them together.

2. Before turning right side out, lay your top and backing, which have been sewn together on three sides, right side down on a large, clean, flat surface. If you don't have a large enough floor space, lay it on as large a table as you can, with the open, unseamed end hanging over the edge of the table, and the bottom half of the quilt lying flat on the table. Place the polyester fiberfill on top and trim it to the exact size of the quilt.

3. Starting at the end opposite the opening, roll the entire quilt, like a sleeping bag, or jelly roll, until you have a long "tube" of fabric and batting (Fig. 2-17).

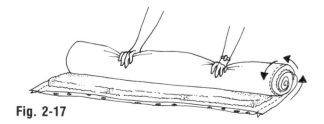

Fig. 2-17

4. Carefully reach inside the layers of fabric (between the face and backing), and slowly pull the tube inside-out, through the opening (Fig. 2-18).

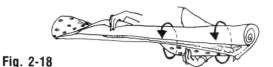

Fig. 2-18

5. Slowly unwrap the quilt (Fig. 2-19), which will open, filled with fiberfill, and with three of the edges finished. (Practice with a sock. First, roll the sock, starting at the toe, and pull the cuff back over the roll. Slowly unroll it from the inside out,

reaching inside the sock, between the layers, and pulling gently on the roll.)

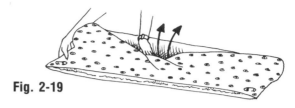

Fig. 2-19

6. Lay the quilt on a large, flat surface, and pin or baste through all layers. Hand or machine quilt, or tie it, as described above.

7. Turn the remaining edges to the inside, pin to hold, and machine stitch to close.

Make a Crib Quilt (42″ × 52″)

Materials Needed

Fabric

Fabric 1, 1¾ yards
Fabric 2, 1⅓ yards
Fabric 3, ¾ yard

Batting and Backing

Backing fabric: 1¾ yards of 44/45″ wide fabric
Polyester fiberfill: 44″ × 54″

Don't Forget

Thread (for piecing your quilt face, as well as for hand or machine quilting, if desired)
String, yarn, or 1/16″ ribbon for tying your quilt, if you prefer
Graph paper or plain paper (which you have scored with 1″ squares) for pattern making

Note: The crib quilt is made of *one* Ohio Star plus side strips (Fig. 2-20). You will need only two pattern pieces.

1. Make your pattern pieces in the dimensions given on the pattern guides on pages 2-15 and 2-16. See "Making the Pattern" in the instructions for the large quilts.

2. Before cutting the patchwork pieces, cut the side strips as follows: Fabric 1 cut two strips 8″ ×

Fig. 2-20

38″ and two strips 4″ × 58″. From Fabric 2 cut two strips 8″ × 30″ and two strips 4″ × 45″.

3. Cut out your fabric patchwork pieces (see pattern guides).

4. Lay out your triangles (Fabrics 1 and 3) as shown in Fig. 2-3, page 2-5. With a ⅜″ seam allowance, piece them as shown in Figs. 2-4 through 2-6.

5. Now arrange your pieced squares and solid squares (Fabrics 2 and 3) as shown in Fig. 2-7. Sew them together in rows, then sew the three rows together to finish your quilt center (Fig. 2-8).

6. Follow the instructions for "Sewing on the Side Strips" and "Finishing the Quilt" in the instructions for the large quilts. The "Alternate Method of Finishing" is particularly nice when used on the crib quilt.

Make a Wall Hanging (36″ square)

Materials Needed

Fabric

Fabric 1, 1¼ yards
Fabric 2, 1 yard
Fabric 3, ¾ yard

Batting and Backing

Polyester fiberfill: 36″ square
Backing fabric: 1¼ yards, cut to fit face of wall hanging

Don't Forget

Thread (for piecing your quilt face, as well as for hand or machine quilting, if desired)
String, yarn, or ¹⁄₁₆″ ribbon for tying your quilt, if you prefer
Graph paper or plain paper (which you have scored with 1″ squares) for pattern making

Note: The wall hanging quilt is made of *one* Ohio Star plus side strips. You will need only two pattern pieces.

1. Make your pattern pieces in the dimensions given in the pattern guides on pages 2-15 and 2-16. See "Making the Pattern" in the instructions for the large quilts.

2. Before cutting the patchwork pattern pieces, cut the side strips as follows: From Fabric 1 cut two strips 3″ × 35″ and two strips 3″ × 40″. From Fabric 2 cut two strips 3″ × 31″ and two strips 3″ × 35″.

3. Cut out your fabric patchwork pieces according to the instructions on the pattern guides on pages 2-15 and 2-16.

4. Lay out your triangles (Fabrics 1 and 3) as shown in Fig. 2-3, page 2-5. With a ⅜″ seam allowance, piece them as shown in Figs. 2-4 through 2-6.

5. Now arrange your pieced squares and solid squares (Fabrics 2 and 3) as shown in Fig. 2-7. Sew

them together in rows, then sew the three rows together to finish your quilt center (Fig. 2-8).

6. Follow the instructions for "Sewing on the Side Strips" and "Finishing the Quilt" in the instructions for the large quilts. The "Alternate Method of Finishing" is particularly nice when used on the wall hanging.

You will probably want to make loops of fabric to sew to the top of the wall hanging or just behind the upper edge (hidden) to allow for a dowel rod to hang it.

To Make the Loops

For **hidden loops**, cut three pieces of fabric 1½″ × 4″. Fold the long edges inward to meet at the center, then fold the whole strip in half lengthwise. Using a straight stitch, sew through all layers along the "open" edge to make a small "ribbon" of fabric. Attach one in the middle of the upper edge of the wall hanging, and the remaining two at either side on the upper edge (Fig. 2-21). Tack these to the wall hanging through all layers using your sewing machine or hand sew them in place.

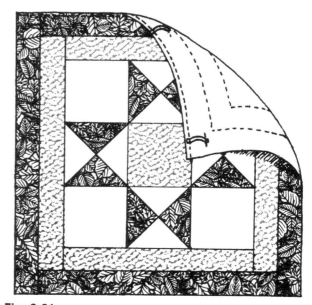

Fig. 2-21

For **decorative loops**, cut three pieces of matching fabric 3″ × 5″. Fold these in half, right sides together, to create 1½″ × 5″ pieces. Using a ⅜″ seam allowance, sew a straight line down the 5″ raw edge. Turn these tubes right side out and press so the seam is centered on one side. Fold these in half widthwise to hide the seam. Attach to the top of your wall hanging by machine, spacing the loops evenly.

For **bow loops**, cut three pieces of wide ribbon, each 24″ long. Fold these in half and tack them to the top edge of your wall hanging by hand or machine, evenly spaced. Tie these loosely around a decorative pole or dowel rod.

The wall hanging is a perfect size for use as a table topper, lap quilt, or sofa throw.

Make a 16″ Throw Pillow

Fabric Requirements

Face: ⅛–¼ yard each of three fabrics (Fabrics 1, 2 and 3)

Back: ½ yard of a matching fabric or a coordinating solid

Ruffle or cord: ⅝ yard

Note: The pillow quilt top is simply *one* Ohio Star with no side strips. You will need only two pattern pieces.

1. Make your pillow pattern pieces in the dimensions given on the pattern guides on pages 2-15 and 2-16. See "Making the Pattern" in the instructions for the large quilts.

2. Cut out your fabric pieces according to the instructions on the pattern guides.

3. Lay out your triangles (Fabrics 1 and 3) as shown in Fig. 2-3, page 2-5. With a ⅜″ seam allowance, piece them as shown in Figs. 2-4 through 2-6.

4. Now arrange your solid squares (Fabrics 2 and 3) and pieced squares as shown in Fig. 2-7. Sew them together in rows, then sew the three rows together to finish your pillow face (Fig. 2-8).

5. You may quilt the pillow face before constructing the pillow. If so, layer it with a backing and fiberfill cut to the same size as the face, then hand or machine quilt along the seams. It is not necessary to quilt the pillow; this is a matter of preference.

6. See the instructions for making ruffling and bias cording on page 2-13. With raw edges together and with a ⅜″ seam allowance, sew bias cording or a ruffle around the entire pillow face. The raw edges of the cording or ruffling match the raw edges of the pillow face (Fig. 2-22). You will need about 2 yards of bias cording or finished ruffling to

go around the pillow. For a knife-edge pillow, with no extra trim, you can eliminate this step.

Fig. 2-22

7. Cut two pieces of backing fabric, 10″ × 17″. Finish one 17″ edge on each of these two pieces with a double ¼″ folded hem, machine stitched.

8. Lay the pillow right side up, with ruffle or cording toward the center. Place the backing right side down on the pillow, overlapping the finished edges evenly in the center. Pin around the edges (Fig. 2-23).

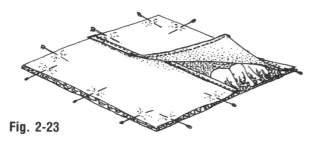

Fig. 2-23

9. Sew around the entire pillow, following the seam used to sew the cording or ruffle in place, or using a ⅜″ seam allowance. Turn inside out through the overlapped backing. Trim away any excess around the seams before turning.

10. Insert a 15″ or 16″ pillow form.

Make a Removable Chair Pad Cover

Note: An additional ⅓ yard of one of the fabrics is required for each chair pad.

1. Complete the 16″ pillow cover as explained in "Make a 16″ Throw Pillow."

2. Cut two strips of fabric, 44″ × 5″. With a roll-hem attachment for your sewing machine, or a narrow double fold, hem around all sides of both strips. Fold each in half, matching the two short ends, to create two tie ends, and pinch or pleat at the fold to gather (Fig. 2-24). At what will be the back two corners, machine stitch the ties to the pillow cover, on the underside of the finished pillow, under the ruffle (Fig. 2-25).

Fig. 2-24

3. To make a removable chair pad insert, purchase or make a 15″–16″ pillow form. With a long needle and double heavy-duty thread, run the thread through the center of the pillow form, leav-

Fig. 2-25

ing a "tail" of thread about 6″ long. Bring the needle back through about ½″ from the first stitch, and tie the ends of the thread, pulling tightly to form a "tuft" in the center.

Two matching chair pads make a lovely rocker set.

Make a Standard Pillow Sham

Fabric Requirements

Face: ½ yard each of Fabric 1 and Fabric 2; ¼ yard of Fabric 3

Back: ⅔ yard (**Note:** If Fabric 3 is used on the face and back, ⅔ yard is enough for both)

Ruffle: ⅞ yard

1. Make your pattern pieces in the dimensions given on the pattern guides on pages 2-15 and 2-16. See "Making the Pattern" in the instructions for the large quilts.

2. Before cutting out your patchwork pattern pieces, cut side strips as follows: From Fabric 2 cut two strips 3½″ × 17″ and two strips 2″ × 23″. From Fabric 1 cut two strips 3½″ × 21″ and two strips 2″ × 29″.

3. Now cut your patchwork pattern pieces out of the appropriate fabrics.

4. To piece the quilt block follow steps 3 and 4 for the 16″ pillow on page 2-11.

5. The side strips will be added to the main quilt block in the same way the strips were added to the large quilt (see Fig. 2-10). Add the 3½″ × 17″ strips of Fabric 2 to opposite sides of the quilt block, trimming away any excess. Add the 2″ × 23″ strips of Fabric 2 in the same manner to the remaining edges. Now add your strips of Fabric 1 the same way.

6. You may wish to first quilt the sham face by layering it with a backing and fiberfill, cut to the same size as the face, then hand or machine quilt along the seams. This is not necessary. It's a matter of preference.

7. See below for instructions on making ruffling and bias cording. With raw edges together, sew bias cording and/or a ruffle around the entire sham face. You will need about 3 yards of bias cording or finished ruffling to go around the pillow sham. (This is sewn to the face side of the pillow sham.)

8. Cut two pieces of backing fabric, 16″ × 24″, finishing one 24″ edge on each piece with a narrow double-folded hem, machine stitched.

9. Lay the pillow sham right side up, with ruffle pressed toward the center. Place the backing right side down on the sham, overlapping the finished edges evenly in the center. Pin around the edges (see Fig. 2-23). Flip it over.

10. Sew around the entire pillow sham, following the seam used to sew ruffling and/or cording in place. Turn inside out through the overlapped backing. Trim away any excess around the seams before turning right-side out (Fig. 2-26).

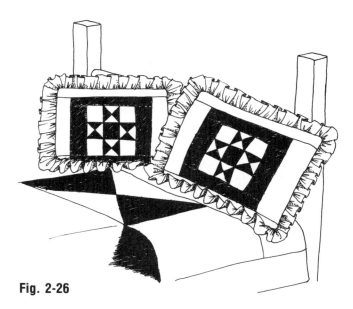

Fig. 2-26

How to Make Matching Ruffling and Bias Cording for Pillows, Shams, and Chair Pads

Ruffling

You will need about ⅝ yard of extra fabric for ruffles around pillows and chair pads. You will need about ⅞ yard for pillow shams.

1. From the width of the fabric (44/45″) cut three 7″ strips (four for pillow shams), and sew them together on the short ends to make a long circle of fabric (Fig. 2-27). Press the seam allowances open.

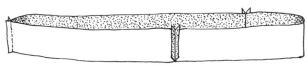

Fig. 2-27

2. Fold the circle in half lengthwise so the raw edges meet and right sides face out. Press.

3. With a wide basting stitch, sew about ¼″ from the raw edge.

4. Divide the circle equally into quarters, identifying the quarter marks with a straight pin. Pin the circle to the center of each straight edge on all four sides of your project, using the pins that mark the quarters to hold the ruffle in place.

5. Pull the basting stitch until the circle gathers into a ruffle equal to the size of the project you are working on (Fig. 2-28; see also Fig. 2-22). Use

Fig. 2-28

straight pins to hold the ruffle in place around the outer edge of the project as you gather it to fit.

Bias Cording

You will need ⅝ yard of matching fabric to make your own bias cording.

1. Cut 1½"-wide strips of fabric on the bias of the fabric. The strip of bias-cut fabric should be several inches longer than the measurement around the edge of the project you wish to trim.

2. Using purchased cording, wrap the bias strip around the cording so that wrong sides and raw edges meet. Using a zipper foot, stitch close to the cord, but not too snug, through both layers of fabric (Fig. 2-29).

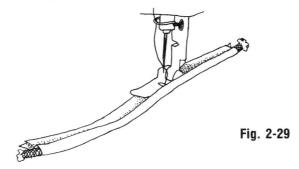

Fig. 2-29

3. The simplest application of the finished bias cording is to begin sewing it on one straight edge, keeping the raw edges of the bias tape and your project even, but with the starting end angled off the edge. Sew around the entire project, clipping the seam allowance of the bias tape at the corners. When you reach your starting point, overlap the bias tape, sewing over the angled end, and carefully angle the final end to sew it off the edge (Fig. 2-30). Clip it to trim.

You may also apply bias tape by starting in the middle of one side, but start your seam about 2" from the end of the bias tape. Sew all around as described above, but when you get to where you started, open the seam on the 2" tail of the bias tape and pull back the fabric to show the cord. Clip off the 2" of cord, and fold the fabric that is left in half, to create a 1" tail (fold the fabric to the inside, so that only the face side shows). Cut the other end of the bias tape so it ends exactly where the first cord now starts. Wrap the folded bias tape fabric around this raw edge, and finish your seam.

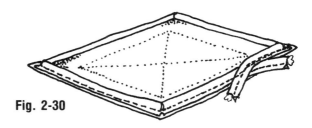

Fig. 2-30

Make a Placemat

Fabric Requirements

Face: ⅛–¼ yard each of three fabrics (Fabrics 1, 2 and 3)

Back: ½ yard of fabric will allow enough for *two* placemats.

1. Make your pattern pieces in the dimensions given on the pattern guides on pages 2-15 and 2-16. See "Making the Pattern" in the instructions for the large quilts.

2. Cut out your patchwork pieces.

3. To piece the quilt block, follow steps 3 and 4 for the 16" pillow on page 2-11.

4. Cut two strips of fabric, 2½" × 17", and sew them to opposite sides of the finished quilt block,

trimming away any excess. Press all seams. This makes the placemat rectangular.

5. Cut a rectangle of backing fabric 17" × 20". Center this, right sides together, on the finished quilt block. Trim excess fabric from the quilt block to equal the size of the backing. Sew together with a ⅜" seam allowance all around, except for a 4" opening centered on one of the seams. Clip the corners and turn inside out through the opening. Hand or machine stitch the opening and press all around.

6. To minimize raveling or fraying of the seams on the inside when these are washed, you may wish to "quilt" along the seam lines, even though these do not have fiberfill. (You may add fiberfill, if you wish.)

Ohio Star Pattern Guides for Large Quilts

Dimensions include ⅜" seam allowance

Note: For large quilts, you will need pattern pieces for a large square, small square, large triangle, and small triangle. Cut these pieces as follows:

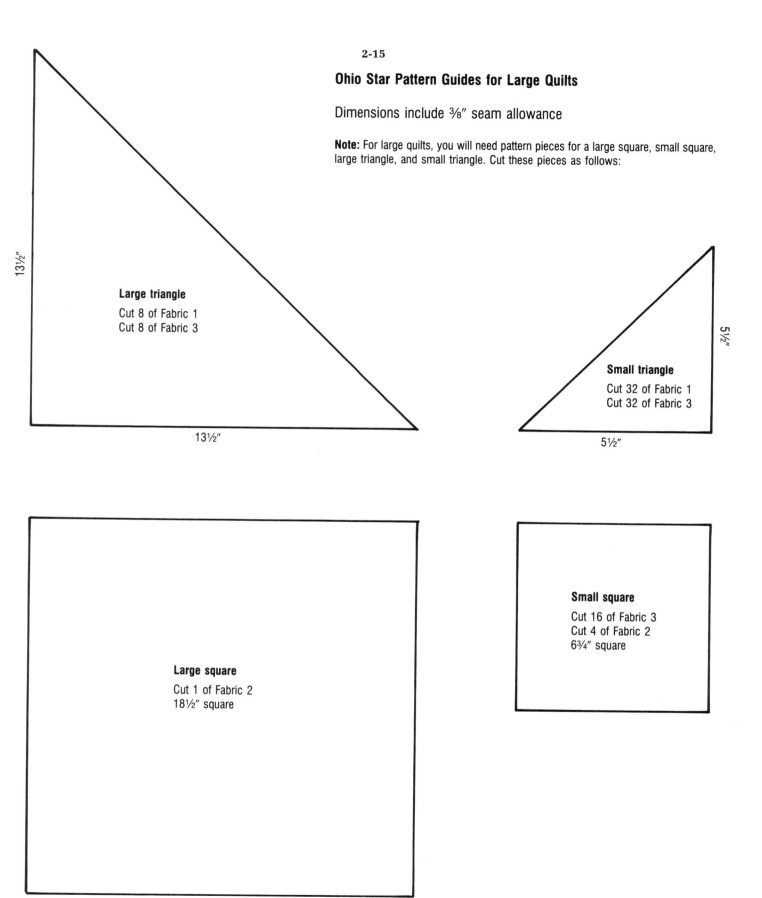

13½"

Large triangle

Cut 8 of Fabric 1
Cut 8 of Fabric 3

13½"

5½"

Small triangle

Cut 32 of Fabric 1
Cut 32 of Fabric 3

5½"

Large square

Cut 1 of Fabric 2
18½" square

Small square

Cut 16 of Fabric 3
Cut 4 of Fabric 2
6¾" square

Note: Instructions for making your templates in the correct dimensions can be found under "Making the Pattern".

Ohio Star Pattern Guides for Crib Quilt, Wall Hanging, Pillow, Pillow Sham, Chair Pad, and Placemat

Dimensions include ⅜″ seam allowance

Note: For crib quilt, wall hanging, pillow, pillow sham, chair pad, and placemat, you will use only one size square and one size triangle. Cut these pieces as follows:

Crib quilt and wall hanging: 7¾″
Pillow, pillow sham, chair pad, and placemat: 5″

Cut 8 of Fabric 1
Cut 8 of Fabric 3

Crib quilt and wall hanging: 7¾″
Pillow, pillow sham, chair pad, and placemat: 5″

Cut 4 of Fabric 3
Cut 1 of Fabric 2

Crib quilt and wall hanging: 10″ square
Pillow, pillow sham, chair pad, and placemat: 6″ square

SUPER SIMPLE QUILTS #3
KATIE'S FAVORITE

Make a Quilt

In this section you will find all the information you need to make a twin, full, queen, or king-size quilt. Instructions for making a crib-size quilt or wall hanging begin on page 3-10.

Getting Started

Katie's Favorite, also known as Goose Tracks, is four pieced blocks, each a "goose track," separated by a pieced cross in the middle. You will get excellent results by using two contrasting prints and a coordinating or light-colored solid fabric. I refer to these as "Fabric 1" (a large print or one with a darker background), "Fabric 2" (a small print or one with a lighter background), and "Fabric 3" (the coordinating solid). (See Fig. 3-4 later in this project.)

Materials Needed

Fabric

Yardage amounts listed below are approximate and will allow for some leftover fabric—enough to make several pillows or two pillow shams or a wall hanging or baby quilt.

Batting and Backing

Polyester fiberfill or wool or cotton batting large enough to complete your quilt.

A large, flat sheet or extra-wide fabric, large enough to use as a backing on your quilt. Three yards of 108″ sheeting (available at well-supplied fabric stores) will fit all sizes. Or, you can use 44/45″ wide fabric as follows: For twin and full sizes, you need 5½ yards of 44/45″ wide fabric, cut into two pieces, each 2¾ yards long. Seam them together along the selvages (Fig. 3-1). For queen and king sizes, you need 8¼ yards of 44/45″ wide fabric, cut in three pieces, each 2¾ yards, seamed together along the selvages (Fig. 3-2).

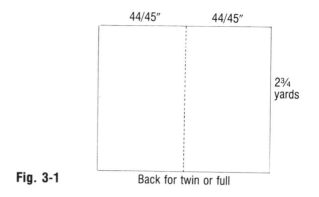

Fig. 3-1 Back for twin or full

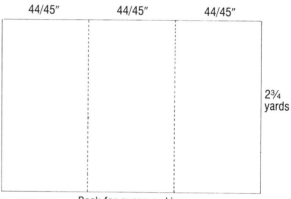

Fig. 3-2 Back for queen or king

When laying out the backing, batting, and quilt top, center the quilt top so the seams in the back are equal distances from the sides.

Don't Forget

Thread (for piecing your quilt face, as well as for hand or machine quilting, if desired)

String, yarn, or ¹⁄₁₆″ ribbon for tying your quilt, if you prefer

Graph paper or plain paper (which you have scored with 1″ squares) for pattern making

	Fabric 1	Fabric 2	Fabric 3
Twin (90″ × 68″)	3½ yards	3 yards	1½ yards
Full (90″ × 76″)	4 yards	3½ yards	1½ yards
Queen (90″ × 90″)	4 yards	3½ yards	1½ yards
King (90″ × 102″)	5 yards	4 yards	1½ yards

Making the Pattern

Making the pattern is as easy as counting squares and connecting dots. The pattern guides on page 3-16 give dimensions for making your own pattern pieces. You may use graph paper, gridded freezer paper, or tracing paper taped to a 1″ gridded cutting board. Graph paper is available in a variety of "squares-to-the-inch" sizes. It doesn't matter what size you choose, as long as the 1″ lines are clearly visible. If you are using smaller pieces of graph paper, carefully tape them together using clear tape, making sure the lines match up vertically and horizontally.

Start by marking a dot on the corner of one square on the grid. This represents one corner of your pattern. Using the 1″ grid on your paper, count, either straight up or down or sideways, exactly the number of inches (squares) indicated on the pattern guide at the end of this project. It helps to have an extra ruler on hand to add a fraction of an inch where needed. Mark another dot when you have reached the number of squares you want, and draw a line between the dots. Continue in this manner until the pattern piece is complete.

Before drawing your angled lines, first draw the straight horizontal and vertical lines. Then just connect the ends of these lines to create the angled line to complete your pattern piece.

When drawing a parallelogram (see pattern guide B on page 3-16), start by marking your first dot (Dot 1) as described above, then mark Dot 2 at the end of the longest line (solid line *plus* dashed line). Draw in the solid line, starting it at Dot 1, but counting squares (inches) to Dot 3 (the end of the solid line). Now draw a dashed line from Dot 2 to Dot 4 (it will be the same length as the dashed line between Dot 3 and Dot 2). Now draw your line between Dot 5 and Dot 4 (it will be the same length as the line between Dot 1 and Dot 3) and complete your parallelogram by connecting Dots 1 and 5, and Dots 3 and 4.

Do not add seam allowances! Unlike in some quilt pattern books, these patterns already include a ³⁄₈″ seam allowance.

After you have drawn your pattern pieces on the grid, double-check all measurements, and carefully cut them out (Fig. 3-3).

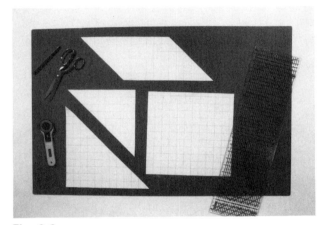

Fig. 3-3

Cutting the Fabric

Rotary cutting tools are ideal for cutting your strips and pattern pieces. Before cutting the patchwork pattern pieces, cut the side strips as follows:

Bed size	Fabric 1	Fabric 2
Twin	2 each, 11″ × 66″	2 each, 11″ × 56″
	2 each, 5″ × 98″	2 each, 5″ × 78″
Full	2 each, 11″ × 76″	2 each, 11″ × 56″
	2 each, 8″ × 98″	2 each, 8″ × 78″
Queen	2 each, 11″ × 78″	2 each, 11″ × 56″
	2 each, 10″ × 98″	2 each, 10″ × 78″
King	2 each, 11″ × 84″	2 each, 11″ × 56″
	2 each, 14″ × 98″	2 each, 14″ × 78″

Note: The center pattern of the quilt is the same for all four bed sizes. The variation in quilt size comes from the different sizes used in the side strips, which are added after the quilt center is pieced. The strip sizes shown above are generous to allow for slight variations in seam allowances or stretch of the fabric. You may trim away the excess after the strip is sewn in place.

After you have cut the long strips of fabric, cut the remaining pattern pieces. The number of pieces needed are shown on the pattern guides on page 3-16. Note that four of each eight pieces for B must be reversed.

Sewing the Main Quilt Block

Hint #1: When one or both pattern pieces are being sewn on a bias (angle-cut) edge, it helps to pin the edges together to prevent pulling or stretching the fabric. Otherwise, it is not necessary to pin pieces together before sewing them. In fact, it's quicker and easier not to. Just be sure you're letting the machine do the work, and that you're not pulling, or "force-guiding," the fabric, which causes bias-cut fabrics to stretch or distort. You can also eliminate this potential problem by using a walking foot on your sewing machine.

Hint #2: Don't worry if your edges don't match perfectly when you are sewing them together. The seams are hidden inside the quilt. And the quilting stitches or ties help camouflage minor flaws. It's the total finished look that will make you proud to give or display your handiwork.

Hint #3: As you work, press all seam allowances toward the darker of the fabrics. This prevents seam allowances from being noticeable through lighter-colored fabrics.

1. After cutting out all pattern pieces, lay the pieces of one corner, or "goose track," of the quilt on a table or on the floor near your sewing machine (Fig. 3-4). Use this layout as a guide for sewing the other three "goose tracks," and sew your guide pieces last.

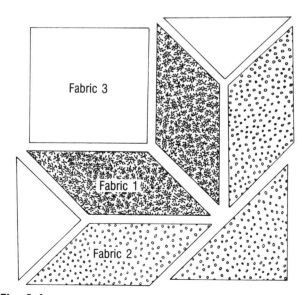

Fig. 3-4

2. Sew piece B, Fabric 1 (shown as B-1 in the drawings) to piece A, Fabric 3 (A-3) (Fig. 3-5). Stop the seam about ⅜″ before the bottom end.

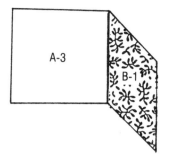

Fig. 3-5

3. Sew piece C to piece B, Fabric 1 (Fig. 3-6). Stop your seam about ⅜″ from the inside point of the triangle.

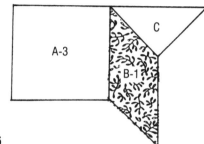

Fig. 3-6

4. Sew piece B, Fabric 2, to piece C, again leaving about ⅜″ unsewn at the inner point (Fig. 3-7). Now fold triangle C in half so the B pieces are right sides together, and sew a seam from the point of the triangle downward to join them.

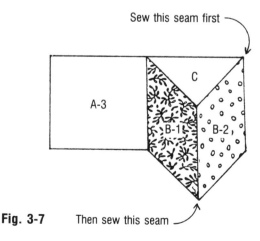

Fig. 3-7

5. Continue in this manner on the perpendicular side of piece A, as shown in Figs. 3-8 through 3-10. Remember that the B pieces are reversed for this side.

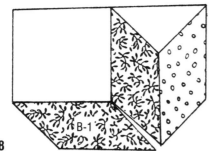

Fig. 3-8

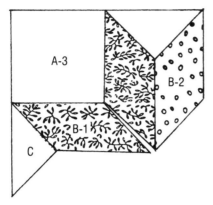

Fig. 3-9

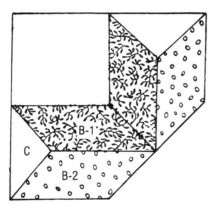

Fig. 3-10

6. Sew the seam that joins the two B pieces (Fabric 1) by folding Square A, Fabric 1, in half on an angle.

7. Sew piece D to pieces B (Fabric 2) to complete one corner block (Fig. 3-11).

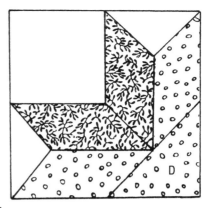

Fig. 3-11

8. Repeat these steps to finish four corner blocks or "goose tracks."

9. Sew piece A, Fabric 3, to piece A, Fabric 1. Arrange two completed corner blocks, or goose tracks, on opposite sides of this piece (Fig. 3-12).

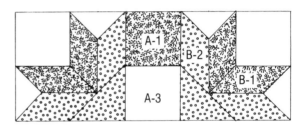

Fig. 3-12

10. Repeat Steps 8 and 9 for the other two goose tracks.

11. Sew the remaining A pieces (Fabrics 1 and 3), starting and ending with Fabric 1, and alternating the squares (Fig. 3-13).

Fig. 3-13

12. Sew this strip between the two goose tracks strips, arranging them as shown in the large drawing at the beginning of this project.

13. Press all seams toward the darker fabric.

Sewing on the Side Strips

1. Sew the shorter strips of Fabric 2 to the top and bottom of your finished quilt center. Trim any excess.

2. Sew the longer strips of Fabric 2 to the remaining edges, including in the seam the strips that were already added (creating a large rectangle).

3. Next, sew the shorter strips of Fabric 1 to the top and bottom.

4. Finally, sew the remaining longest strips of Fabric 1 to the last two sides of the quilt to complete the face (Fig. 3-14). Press all seams toward dark.

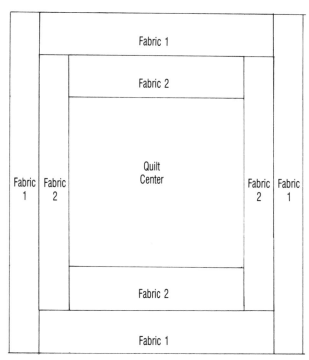

Fig. 3-14

Finishing the Quilt

1. Cut and seam the backing fabric, if necessary, to equal the size of your finished quilt top (see Figs. 3-1, 3-2).

2. Lay the backing (sheet, sheeting, or seamed fabric) right side down on a large, clean surface.

3. Place the polyester fiberfill or other batting on top of the backing.

4. Lay the quilt top right side up on the fiberfill. Hand baste, or pin using large safety pins, through all layers to hold them in place. (I prefer safety pins to straight pins because they save my hands and other body parts from pinpricks as I work.)

5. Using yarn, string, or ¹⁄₁₆″ ribbon, tie the layers firmly, or quilt the layers by hand or machine, as desired. Instructions follow.

6. Finish the edges, using bias tape or other decorative trim, as desired (Fig. 3-15). (Instructions follow.) The edges can also be turned easily to the inside and sewn in place by machine (Fig. 3-16). You can insert piping, lace, or a ruffle at the edge with this method.

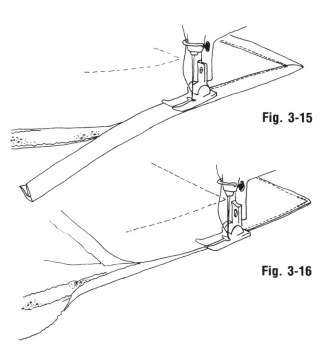

Fig. 3-15

Fig. 3-16

To Add Bias Tape

There are many ways to apply a bias taped edge, but, in general, it is easiest if you sew a seam around your entire project, using a narrow seam allowance, to keep the layers from stretching or shifting *before* you apply the bias tape.

Starting in the middle of one side of your project, and using long straight pins, pin the bias tape around the entire piece, overlapping and folding under the last edge where it meets with your starting point. When you get to a corner, tuck the excess flatly and neatly inside of itself, by gently pushing it to one side with pointed scissors or a pin. It may help to open the bias tape so it is flat when you get to a corner, then pinch the excess to guide it into the fold at the corner (Fig. 3-17). Hand baste or topstitch by machine over the miter.

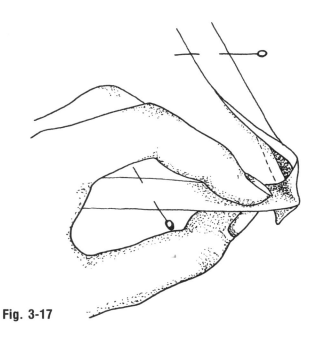

Fig. 3-17

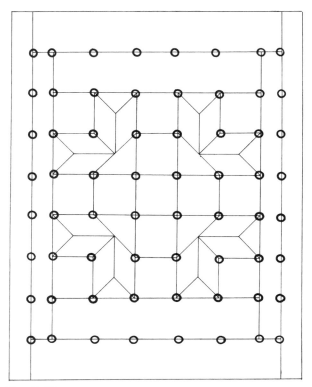

Fig. 3-18

There are a number of quilt books available with chapters devoted to finishing the edges of your quilt. Some books have been written solely on the subject. Your local library or bookstore should have a variety of books to choose from.

To Tie Your Quilt

Tying your quilt is the easiest method of holding the layers together and provides a quick finish to your quilt. Baste or pin the layers of your quilt to hold them in place before starting to tie. It is not necessary to mark the points at which you will tie your quilt. Figure 3-18 shows where the ties should be placed.

Thread a large needle (one with a large eye, such as a tapestry needle) with yarn, 1/16" ribbon, or string (button or quilting thread also works well). Working from the top of the quilt, push the needle through all layers, drawing the thread through, but not all the way. Leave a 6"–8" tail sticking out on top. About 1/8"–1/4" from the first stitch, draw the needle back up (from the back to the front) through all layers. Cut the thread, again leaving a tail about 6"–8" long. Tie these two tails tightly together, using a double or triple knot to hold the tie securely in place. You can make a bow with the excess, or simply trim the tails to about 1".

To Quilt by Machine

After the layers are securely pinned or basted, roll up one-half of the quilt tightly enough to allow it to fit under the head of your sewing machine. You can safety-pin it closed or use bicycle clips to hold the roll. With larger quilts, you may need a friend to help guide the bulk through while you are quilting the center block.

Starting with the seams shown in Fig. 3-19, stitch "anchoring" quilt lines to hold all layers in place. This stitching will secure all layers of fabric and help keep the remainder of the quilt from shifting. It also helps to smooth the top and bottom toward you occasionally, with one hand above and one hand below, palms pressed gently together, and fingers spread.

After you have stitched the lines shown in Fig. 3-19, continue quilting by machine, following the outline of the pattern by sewing along the seam lines of the pieced quilt top. Be sure to back-tack the beginning and end of each quilting seam. I like to use thread that matches one of the lighter fabrics. When quilting along a seam that joins a solid color to a print fabric, try to keep your quilting stitches on the printed fabric, to the side of the seam.

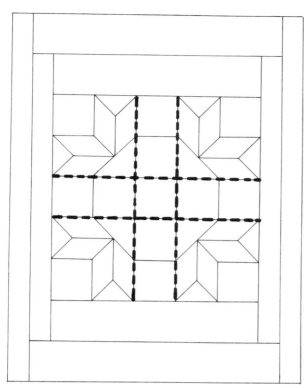

Fig. 3-19

Today's polyester fiberfills don't clump or shift as much as natural battings, like wool or cotton, because of the resins that hold the polyester fibers together. The stitching lines suggested here are adequate to hold polyester fiberfill in place, but you may wish to add some extra quilting lines or ties if you are using pure wool or cotton batting.

Alternate Method of Finishing

1. Another method of finishing your quilt is to sew the face to the backing, right sides together, leaving the top edge open. Because these seams are so long, it helps to pin the edges together before sewing, to hold them in place. Be sure the back is cut to the exact size of the face before sewing them together.

2. Before turning right side out, lay your top and backing, which have been sewn together on three sides, right side down on a large, clean, flat surface. If you don't have a large enough floor space, lay it on as large a table as you can, with the open, unseamed end hanging over the edge of the table, and the bottom half of the quilt lying flat on the table. Place the polyester fiberfill on top and trim it to the exact size of the quilt.

3. Starting at the end opposite the opening, roll the entire quilt, like a sleeping bag, or jelly roll, until you have a long "tube" of fabric and batting.

4. Carefully reach inside the layers of fabric (between the face and backing), and slowly pull the tube inside-out, through the opening (Fig. 3-20).

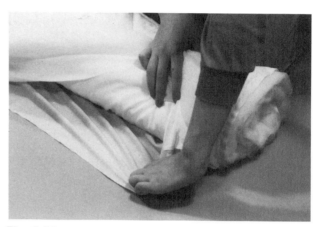

Fig. 3-20

5. Slowly unwrap the quilt (Fig. 3-21), which will open, filled with fiberfill, and with three of the edges finished. (Practice with a sock. First, roll the sock, starting at the toe, and pull the cuff back over the roll. Slowly unroll it from the inside out, reaching inside the sock, between the layers, and pulling gently on the roll.)

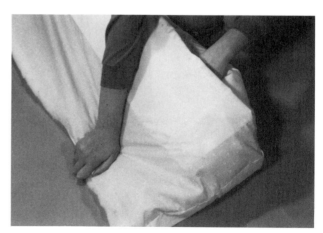

Fig. 3-21

6. Lay the quilt on a large, flat surface, and pin or baste through all layers. Hand or machine quilt, or tie it, as described above.

7. Turn the remaining edges to the inside, pin to hold, and machine stitch to close.

Make a Crib Quilt (42″ × 52″)

Materials Needed

Fabric

Fabric 1, 1¾ yards
Fabric 2, 1⅓ yards
Fabric 3, ⅓ yard

Batting and Backing

Polyester fiberfill: 44″ × 54″
Backing fabric: 1¾ yards of 44/45″ wide fabric

Don't Forget

Thread (for piecing your quilt face, as well as for hand or machine quilting, if desired)
String, yarn, or 1⁄16″ ribbon for tying your quilt, if you prefer

Graph paper or plain paper (which you have scored with 1″ squares) for pattern making

1. Make your pattern pieces in the dimensions given on the pattern guides on page 3-16. See "Making the Pattern" in the instructions for the large quilts.

2. Before cutting the patchwork pieces, cut the side strips as follows: From Fabric 1, cut two strips 8″ × 38″ and two strips 4″ × 58″. From Fabric 2, cut two strips 8″ × 30″ and two strips 4″ × 45″.

3. Cut out your fabric patchwork pieces.

4. Follow the instructions in "Sewing the Main Quilt Block," "Sewing on the Side Strips," and "Finishing the Quilt" to complete the crib quilt. (This pattern is simply a miniature version of the large quilt.) The "Alternate Method of Finishing" is particularly nice when used on the crib quilt.

Make a Wall Hanging (36″ square)

Materials Needed

Fabric

Fabric 1, 1¼ yards
Fabric 2, 1 yard
Fabric 3, ⅓ yard

Batting and Backing

Polyester fiberfill: 36″ square
Backing fabric: 1¼ yards, cut to fit face of wall hanging

Don't Forget

Thread (for piecing your quilt face, as well as for hand or machine quilting, if desired)
String, yarn, or 1⁄16″ ribbon for tying your quilt, if you prefer
Graph paper or plain paper (which you have scored with 1″ squares)

1. Make your pattern pieces in the dimensions given in the pattern guides on page 3-16. See "Making the Pattern" in the instructions for the large quilts.

2. Before cutting the patchwork pattern pieces, cut the side strips as follows: From Fabric 1, cut two strips 3″ × 35″ and two strips 3″ × 40″. From Fabric 2, cut two strips 3″ × 31″ and two strips 3″ × 35″.

3. Cut out your fabric patchwork pieces.

4. Follow the instructions in "Sewing the Main Quilt Block," "Sewing on the Side Strips," and "Finishing the Quilt" to complete the wall hanging. (This pattern is simply a miniature version of the large quilt.) The "Alternate Method of Finishing" is particularly nice when used on the wall hanging.

You will probably want to make loops of fabric to sew to the top of the wall hanging or just behind the upper edge (hidden) to allow for a dowel rod to hang it.

To Make the Loops

For **hidden loops**, cut three pieces of fabric 1½″ × 4″. Fold the long edges inward to meet at the center, then fold the whole strip in half length-wise. Using a straight stitch, sew through all layers along the "open" edge to make a small "ribbon" of fabric. Attach one in the middle of the upper edge of the wall hanging, and the remaining two at either side on the upper edge. Tack these to the wall hanging through all layers using your sewing machine, or hand sew them in place.

For **decorative loops**, cut three pieces of matching fabric 3″ × 5″. Fold these in half, right sides together, to create 1½″ × 5″ pieces. Using a ⅜″ seam allowance, sew a straight line down the 5″ raw edge. Turn these tubes right side out and press so the seam is centered on one side. Fold these in half widthwise to hide the seam. Attach to the top of your wall hanging by machine, spacing the loops evenly.

For **bow loops**, cut three pieces of wide ribbon, each 24″ long. Fold these in half and tack them to the top edge of your wall hanging by hand or machine, evenly spaced. Tie these loosely around a decorative pole or dowel rod (Fig. 3-22).

The wall hanging is a perfect size for use as a table topper, lap quilt, or sofa throw.

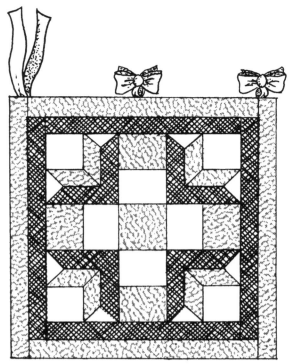

Fig. 3-22

Make a 16″ Throw Pillow

Fabric Requirements

Face: ⅛–¼ yard each of three fabrics (Fabrics 1, 2, and 3)

Back: ½ yard of a matching fabric or a coordinating solid

Ruffle or cord: ⅝ yard

1. Make your pattern pieces in the dimensions given on the pattern guides on page 3-16. See "Making the Pattern" in the instructions for the large quilts.

2. Cut out your fabric pieces according to the instructions on the pattern guides.

3. Follow the steps in "Sewing the Main Quilt Block" in the instructions for the large quilts. (You will not add side strips.)

4. You may quilt the pillow face before constructing the pillow if you wish (although this is not necessary). If you do, layer it with a backing and fiberfill cut to the same size as the face, then hand or machine quilt along the seams.

5. See the instructions on page 3-14 on making and applying ruffling and bias cording. With raw edges together and with a ⅜″ seam allowance, sew bias cording (Fig. 3-23) or a ruffle (Fig. 3-24) around the entire pillow face. You will need about 2 yards of bias cording or finished ruffling to go around the pillow. For a knife-edge pillow, with no extra trim, you can eliminate this step.

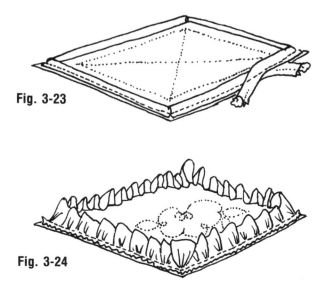

Fig. 3-23

Fig. 3-24

6. Cut two pieces of backing fabric, 10″ × 17″. Finish one 17″ edge on each of these two pieces with a double-folded hem, machine stitched.

7. Lay the pillow right side up, with ruffle or cording toward the center. Place the backing right side down on the pillow, overlapping the finished edges evenly in the center. Pin around the edges (Fig. 3-25).

8. Sew around the entire pillow, following the seam used to sew the cording or ruffle in place, or using a ⅜″ seam allowance. Turn inside out

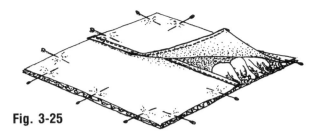

Fig. 3-25

through the overlapped backing. Trim away any excess around the seams before turning.

9. Insert a 15″ or 16″ pillow form.

Make Your Own 15″–16″ Pillow Form

1. Save your scrap fiberfill.

2. Cut two 18″ squares of any white or ivory fabric.

3. Sew these together on three sides, using a ½″ seam allowance. Turn right side out.

4. Cut two 17″ squares of leftover fiberfill, and carefully slide them into the pillow cover. Con-

tinue to stuff smaller bits of fiberfill between the squares, until the pillow is plump, but not too hard.

5. To finish, whipstitch the opening by hand. I call this a 15″–16″ finished size because the finished size will vary according to the plumpness of the pillow.

Make a Removable Chair Pad Cover

Note: An additional ⅓ yard of one of the fabrics is required for each chair pad.

1. Complete the 16″ pillow cover as explained in "Make a 16″ Throw Pillow."

2. Cut two strips of fabric, 44″ × 5″. With a roll-hem attachment for your sewing machine, or a narrow double fold, hem around all sides of both strips. You may wish to fold one corner of each end to the inside and machine stitch to hold in place, to create pointed ends. Fold each in half, matching the two short ends, to create two tie ends, and pinch or pleat at the fold to gather. At what will be the back two corners, machine stitch the ties to the pillow cover, on the underside of the finished pillow, under the ruffle (Fig. 3-26).

3. To make a removable chair pad insert, purchase or make a 15″–16″ pillow form. With a long needle and double heavy-duty thread, run the thread through the center of the pillow form, leav-

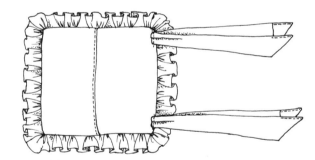

Fig. 3-26

ing a "tail" of thread about 6″ long. Bring the needle back through about ½″ from the first stitch, and tie the ends of the thread, pulling tightly to form a "tuft" in the center.

Two matching chair pads with inserts make a lovely rocker set.

Make a Standard Pillow Sham

Fabric Requirements

Face: ½ yard each of Fabric 1 and Fabric 2; ¼ yard of Fabric 3

Back: ⅔ yard (**Note:** If Fabric 3 is used on the face and back, ⅔ yard is enough for both)

Ruffle: ⅞ yard

1. Make your pattern pieces in the dimensions given on the pattern guides on page 3-16. See "Making the Pattern" in the instructions for the large quilts. Cut all fabric pieces according to the instructions on the pattern guides.

2. Follow the piecing instructions under "Sewing the Main Quilt Block" in the instructions for the large quilts.

3. Cut two strips of Fabric 2, 3½″ × 17″, and two strips 2″ × 23″.

4. Cut two strips of Fabric 1, 3½″ × 21″, and two strips 2″ × 29″.

5. Add the 3½″ × 17″ strips of Fabric 2 to opposite sides of the quilt block, trimming away any excess. Add the 2″ × 23″ strips of the same fabric, in the same manner, to the remaining edges.

6. Add the 3½″ × 21″ strips of Fabric 1 to the first sides (as in Step 5), and add the remaining strips to the last two sides.

7. You may wish to quilt the sham face first, before adding the outer, overlapped backing, by layering it with a plain muslin backing or piece or scrap fabric and fiberfill cut to the same size as the face, then hand or machine quilt along the seams. This is not necessary—simply a matter of preference.

8. See the instructions for making and applying ruffling and bias cording, page 3-14. With raw together, sew bias cording and/or a ruffle around the entire sham face. You will need about 3 yards of bias cording or finished ruffling to go around the pillow sham. (This is sewn to the right side of the pillow sham—See Figs. 3-23, 3-24.)

9. Cut two pieces of a backing fabric, 16″ × 24″, finishing one 24″ edge on each piece with a narrow, double-folded hem, machine stitched.

10. Lay the pillow sham right side up, with ruffle pressed toward the center. Place the backing, face down, on the sham, overlapping the finished edges evenly in the center. Pin around the edges (see Fig. 3-25).

11. Sew around the entire pillow sham, following the seam used to sew ruffling and/or cording in place. Turn inside out through the overlapped backing. Trim away any excess around the seams before turning right-side out (Fig. 3-27).

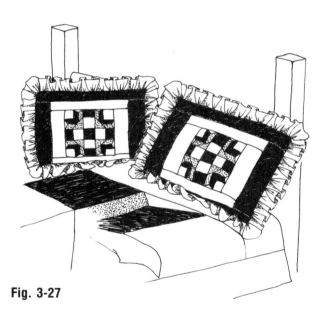

Fig. 3-27

How to Make Matching Ruffling and Bias Cording for Pillows, Shams, and Chair Pads

Ruffling

You will need about ⅝ yard of extra fabric for ruffles around pillows and chair pads. You will need about ⅞ yard for pillow shams.

1. From the width of the fabric (44/45″) cut three 7″ strips (four strips for pillow shams), and sew them together on the short ends to make a long circle of fabric. Press the seam allowances open.

2. Fold the circle in half lengthwise, so the raw edges meet, and right sides face out. Press.

3. With a wide basting stitch, sew about ¼″ from the raw edge (Fig. 3-28).

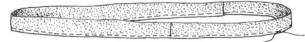

Fig. 3-28

4. Divide the circle equally into quarters, identifying the quarter marks with a straight pin. Pin the circle to the center of each straight edge on all four sides of your project, using the pins that mark the quarters to hold the ruffle in place.

5. Pull the basting stitch until the circle gathers evenly into a ruffle equal to the size of the project you are working on. Use straight pins to hold the ruffle in place around the outer edge of the project, raw edges together, as you gather it to fit.

Bias Cording

You will need ⅝ yard of matching fabric to make your own bias cording.

1. Cut 1½″-wide strips of fabric on the bias of the fabric. The strip of bias-cut fabric should be several inches longer than the measurement around the edge of the project you wish to trim.

2. Using purchased cording, wrap the bias strip around the cording so that wrong sides and raw edges meet. With a zipper foot attachment, stitch close to the cord, but not too snug, through both layers of fabric (Fig. 3-29).

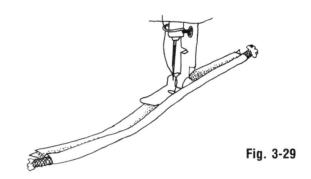

Fig. 3-29

3. The simplest application of the finished bias cording is to begin sewing it on one straight edge, keeping the raw edges of the bias tape and your project even, but with the starting end angled off the edge. Sew around the entire project, clipping the seam allowance of the bias tape at the corners. When you reach your starting point, overlap the bias tape, sewing over the angled end, and carefully angle the final end to sew it off the edge (see Fig. 3-23). Clip it to trim.

You may also apply bias tape by starting in the middle of one side, but start your seam about 2″ from the end of the bias tape. Sew all around as described above, but when you get to where you started, open the seam on the 2″ tail of the bias tape and pull back the fabric to show the cord. Clip off the 2″ of cord, and fold the fabric that is left in half, to create a 1″ tail (fold the fabric to the inside, so that only the right side shows). Cut the other end of the bias tape so it ends exactly where the first cord now starts. Wrap the folded bias tape fabric around this raw edge, and finish your seam.

Make a Placemat

Fabric Requirements

Face: ⅛ to ¼ yard each of three fabrics (Fabrics 1, 2, and 3)

Back: ½ yard of fabric will allow enough for *two* placemats.

1. Make your pattern pieces in the dimensions given on the pattern guides on page 3-16.

2. Cut all fabric pieces according to the instructions on the pattern guides.

3. Follow the piecing instructions under "Sewing the Main Quilt Block" in the instructions for the large quilts.

4. Cut two strips of fabric, 2½″ × 17″, and sew them to opposite sides of the finished quilt block, trimming away any excess. Press all seams.

5. Cut a rectangle of backing fabric 17″ × 20″. Center this, right sides together, on the finished quilt block. Trim excess fabric from the quilt block to equal the size of the backing. Sew together with a ⅜″ seam allowance all around, except for a 4″ opening centered on one of the seams. Clip the corners and turn inside out through the opening. Hand or machine stitch the opening and press all around.

6. To minimize raveling or fraying of the seams on the inside when these are washed, you may wish to "quilt" along the seam lines, even though these do not have fiberfill. (You may add fiberfill, if you wish.)

Katie's Favorite Pattern Guides

Dimensions include ⅜″ seam allowance.

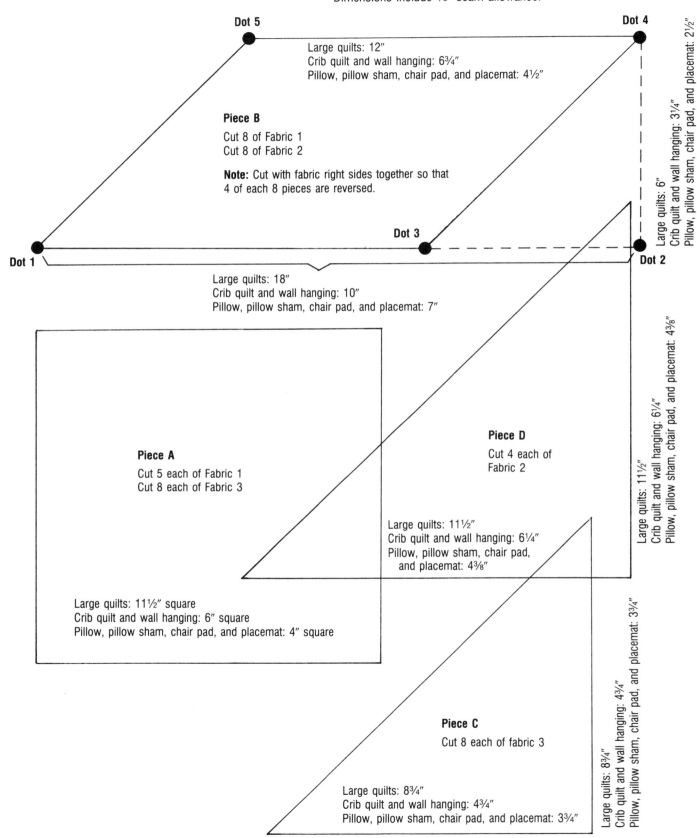

Dot 5

Dot 4

Large quilts: 12″
Crib quilt and wall hanging: 6¾″
Pillow, pillow sham, chair pad, and placemat: 4½″

Large quilts: 2½″
Crib quilt and wall hanging: 3¼″
Pillow, pillow sham, chair pad, and placemat: 2½″

Piece B

Cut 8 of Fabric 1
Cut 8 of Fabric 2

Note: Cut with fabric right sides together so that
4 of each 8 pieces are reversed.

Dot 3

Large quilts: 6″
Crib quilt and wall hanging: 3¼″
Pillow, pillow sham, chair pad, and placemat: 2½″

Dot 1

Dot 2

Large quilts: 18″
Crib quilt and wall hanging: 10″
Pillow, pillow sham, chair pad, and placemat: 7″

Piece D

Cut 4 each of
Fabric 2

Large quilts: 11½″
Crib quilt and wall hanging: 6¼″
Pillow, pillow sham, chair pad,
  and placemat: 4⅜″

Large quilts: 11½″
Crib quilt and wall hanging: 6¼″
Pillow, pillow sham, chair pad, and placemat: 4⅜″

Piece A

Cut 5 each of Fabric 1
Cut 8 each of Fabric 3

Large quilts: 11½″ square
Crib quilt and wall hanging: 6″ square
Pillow, pillow sham, chair pad, and placemat: 4″ square

Large quilts: 8¾″
Crib quilt and wall hanging: 4¾″
Pillow, pillow sham, chair pad, and placemat: 3¾″

Piece C

Cut 8 each of fabric 3

Large quilts: 8¾″
Crib quilt and wall hanging: 4¾″
Pillow, pillow sham, chair pad, and placemat: 3¾″

Note: Instructions for making your templates in the correct dimensions can be found under "Making the Pattern."

SUPER SIMPLE QUILTS #4

FACETS

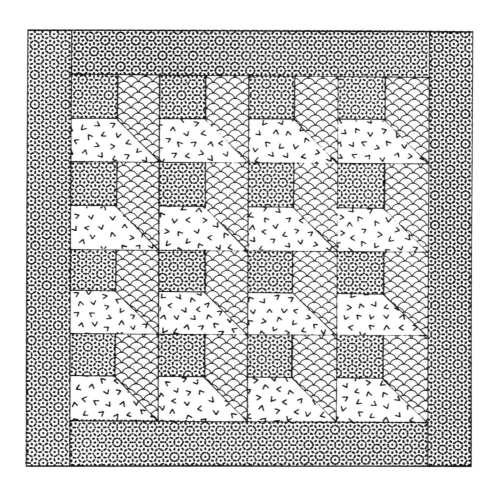

Make a Quilt

In this section you will find all the information you need to make a twin (90″ × 68″), full (90″ × 76″), queen (90″ × 90″), or king-size (90″ × 102″) quilt. Instructions for making a crib-size quilt or wall hanging begin on page 4-9.

Getting Started

Facets, also known as Attic Windows, is composed of three pattern pieces, a square and two trapezoids, arranged to look like a windowsill. This quilt is one of the easiest to make, and can be one of the richest looking, depending on your choice of fabrics. Choose one bold print for the square in the pattern and complementary solid colors or mini-prints for the other fabrics. A plaid or buffalo check flannel combined with two coordinating solid colors makes a wonderful quilt for a boy's or young man's room.

Fabrics are referred to as "Fabric 1" (a print fabric or plaid, or a dark colored solid fabric), "Fabric 2" (a coordinating solid or mini-print), and "Fabric 3" (another coordinating solid or mini-print). (See Fig. 4-4.)

Materials Needed

Fabric

Yardage amounts listed below are approximate, and this pattern does not allow for much, if any, leftover fabric.

For your *quilt center*, you will need the following amount of fabric:

	Fabric 1	Fabric 2	Fabric 3
Twin or full	1 yard	1½ yards	1½ yards
Queen or king	1⅓ yards	2 yards	2 yards

For your *side strips*, you will need an additional 2⅔ yards of *one* of your three fabrics.

Batting and Backing

Polyester fiberfill or wool or cotton batting large enough to complete your quilt.

A large, flat sheet or extra-wide fabric, large enough to use as a backing on your quilt. Three yards of 108″ sheeting (available at well-supplied fabric stores) will fit all sizes. Or you can use 44/45″ wide fabric as follows: For twin and full sizes, you need 5½ yards of 44/45″ wide fabric, cut into two pieces, each 2¾ yards long. Seam them together along the selvages (Fig. 4-1). For queen and king sizes, you need 8¼ yards of 44/45″ wide fabric, cut in three pieces, each 2¾ yards, seamed together along the selvages.

When laying out the backing, batting, and quilt top in preparation for quilting, center the quilt top so the seams in the back are equal distances from the sides.

Don't Forget

Thread (for piecing your quilt face, as well as for hand or machine quilting, if desired)

String, yarn, or 1⁄16″ ribbon for tying your quilt, if you prefer

Graph paper or plain paper (which you have scored with 1″ squares) for pattern making

Making the Pattern

Making the pattern is as easy as counting squares and connecting dots. The pattern guides on pages 4-15 and 4-16 give dimensions for making your own pattern pieces. You may use graph paper, gridded freezer paper, or tracing paper taped to a 1″ gridded cutting board. Graph paper is available in a variety of "squares-to-the-inch"

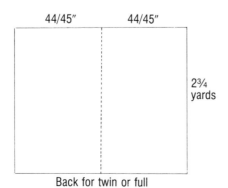

Fig. 4-1

44/45″   44/45″

2¾ yards

Back for twin or full

sizes. It doesn't matter what size you choose, as long as the 1″ lines are clearly visible. If you are using smaller pieces of graph paper, carefully tape them together using clear tape, making sure the lines match up vertically and horizontally.

Start by marking a dot on the corner of one square on the grid. This represents one corner of your pattern. Using the 1″ grid on your paper, count, either straight up or down, or sideways, exactly the number of inches (squares) indicated on the pattern guide at the end of this project. It helps to have an extra ruler on hand to add a fraction of an inch where needed. Mark another dot when you have reached the number of squares you want, and draw a line between the dots. Continue in this manner until the pattern piece is complete.

Before drawing your angled lines, first draw the straight horizontal and vertical lines. Then just connect the ends of these lines to create the angled line to complete your pattern piece.

Do not add seam allowances! Unlike in some quilt pattern books, these patterns already include a ⅜″ seam allowance.

After you have drawn your pattern pieces on the grid, double-check all measurements, and carefully cut them out (Fig. 4-2).

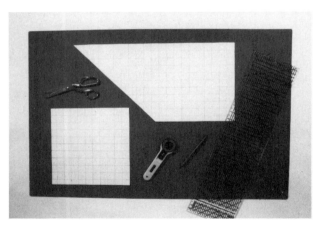

Fig. 4-2

Cutting the Fabric

Rotary cutting tools are ideal for cutting your strips and pattern pieces. Before cutting the patchwork pattern pieces, cut the side strips as follows: From the 2⅔-yard piece of fabric purchased for use on the side strips, cut two strips as follows:

Twin: two strips 6″ × 64″ and two strips 6″ × 94″
Full: two strips 6″ × 64″ and two strips 11″ × 94″
Queen: two strips 6″ × 84″ and two strips 6″ × 94″
King: two strips 6″ × 84″ and two strips 14″ × 94″

Note: The center pattern of the quilt is the same for the twin and full sizes, and the same for the queen and king sizes. The variation in quilt size comes from the different sizes of side strips added after the quilt center is pieced. The strip sizes shown above are generous, to allow for slight variations in seam allowances or stretch of the fabric. You may trim away the excess after the strip is sewn in place.

After you have cut the side strips, cut the remaining pattern pieces. The number of pieces needed is shown on the pattern guides on pages 4-15 and 4-16.

If you are using a fabric that has an obvious right side, please note that all fabric should be cut right side up, not back-to-back or right sides together. **Note:** For the trapezoid piece, although Fabrics 2 and 3 will be cut right side up, the *pattern piece* will be used right side up on one of these fabrics, then flipped over to be reversed on the other. Use Fig. 4-3 as a guide for the most efficient use of your fabric as you cut the trapezoid-shaped pieces.

Fig. 4-3

Sewing the Main Quilt Block

Hint #1: When one or both pattern pieces is being sewn on a bias (angle-cut) edge, it helps to pin the edges together to prevent pulling or stretching the fabric. Otherwise, it is not necessary to pin pieces together before sewing them. In fact, it's quicker and easier not to. Just be sure you're letting the machine do the work, and that you're not pulling, or "force-guiding," the fabric, which causes bias-cut fabrics to stretch or distort. You can also eliminate this potential problem by using a walking foot on your sewing machine.

Hint #2: Don't worry if your edges don't match perfectly when you are sewing them together. The seams are hidden inside the quilt. And the quilting stitches or ties help camouflage minor flaws. It's the total finished look that will make you proud to give or display your handiwork.

Hint #3: As you work, press all seam allowances toward the darker of the fabrics to prevent seam allowances from being noticeable through lighter-colored fabrics.

1. Before sewing, lay out your blocks as shown in Fig. 4-4. Using a ⅜″ seam allowance, sew trapezoid

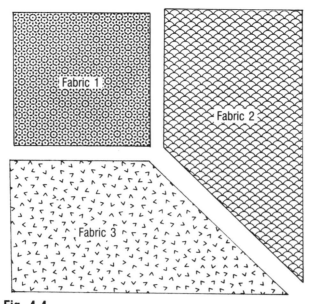

Fig. 4-4

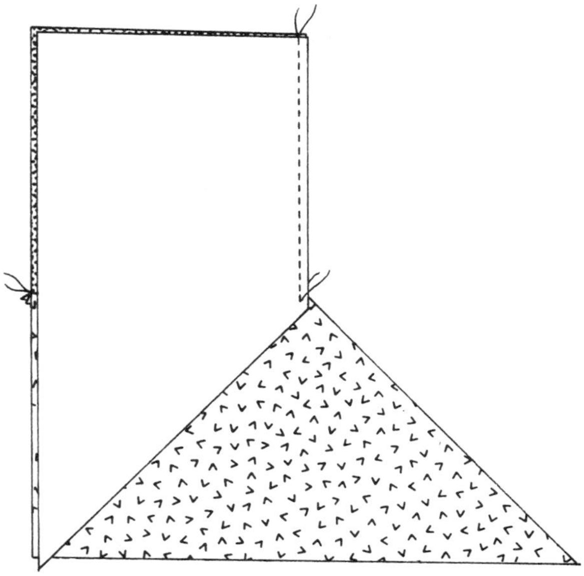

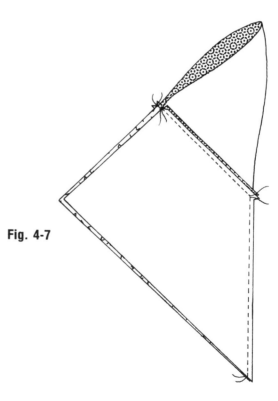

Fig. 4-6

pieces B to square A, stopping ⅜″ from where the trapezoids meet at the corner (Figs. 4-5, 4-6).

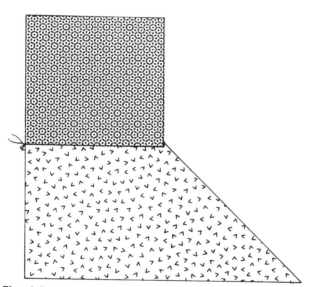

Fig. 4-5

Fig. 4-7

2. To sew the angled seam, fold the entire block in half, right sides together, diagonally through the square piece. Sew from the corner of the square to the points of the trapezoid (Fig. 4-7).

3. Repeat these steps until you have completed all the blocks. Press the seams toward the trapezoids where sewn to the square, and open on the angles of the trapezoids.

4. Lay the blocks so that all squares are in the upper right- or left-hand corner, according to your preference. Sew the squares together in vertical rows of four (Fig. 4-8). Twin and full sizes will have three rows; queen and king sizes will have four rows.

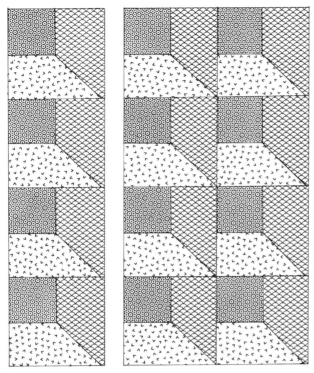

Fig. 4-8

Sewing on the Side Strips

Using a ³⁄₈″ seam allowance, sew the strips to the top and bottom of the finished quilt center in the order shown in Fig. 4-9. Trim the excess length from each strip as it is sewn in place, as some allowance has been built in for slight variations in

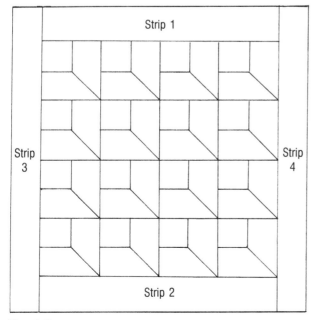

Fig. 4-9

piecing the center area. Next, sew the longer side strips to the sides of the quilt top; including the first two strips that were sewn. Trim excess. Now your quilt top is complete.

Finishing the Quilt

1. Cut and seam the backing fabric, if necessary, to equal the size of your finished quilt top (see page 4-3).

2. Lay the backing (sheet, sheeting, or seamed fabric) right side down on a large, clean surface.

3. Place the polyester fiberfill or other batting on top of the backing.

4. Lay the quilt top right side up on the fiberfill. Hand baste, or pin using large safety pins, through all layers to hold them in place. (I prefer safety pins to straight pins because they save my hands and other body parts from pinpricks as I work.)

5. Using yarn, string, or ¹⁄₁₆″ ribbon, tie the layers firmly, or quilt the layers by hand or machine, as desired. Instructions follow.

6. Finish the edges, using bias tape or other decorative trim, as desired. The edges can also be turned easily to the inside and sewn in place by machine (Fig. 4-10). You can insert piping, lace, or a ruffle at the edge with this method.

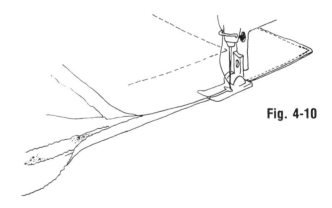

Fig. 4-10

To Add Bias Tape

There are many ways to apply a bias taped edge, but in general, it is easiest if you sew a seam around your entire project, using a narrow seam allowance, to keep the layers from stretching or shifting *before* you apply the bias tape.

Starting in the middle of one side of your project, and using long straight pins, pin the bias tape around the entire piece, overlapping and folding under the last edge where it meets with your starting point. When you get to a corner, tuck the excess flatly and neatly inside of itself, by gently pushing it to one side with pointed scissors or a pin. It may help to open the bias tape so it is flat when you get to a corner, then pinch the excess to guide it into the fold at the corner (Fig. 4-11). Hand baste or topstitch by machine over the miter.

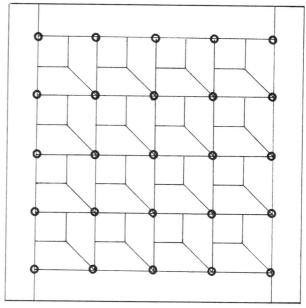

Fig. 4-12

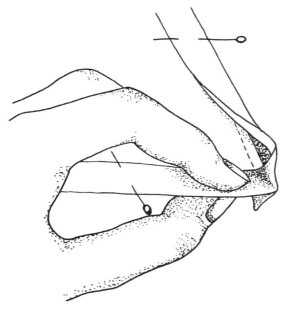

Fig. 4-11

There are a number of quilt books available with chapters devoted to finishing the edges of your quilt. Some books have been written solely on the subject. Your local library or bookstore should have a variety of books to choose from.

To Tie Your Quilt

Tying your quilt is the easiest way to hold the layers together and provides a quick finish to your quilt. Baste or pin the layers of your quilt to hold them in place before you begin. It is not necessary to mark the points at which you will tie your quilt. Figure 4-12 shows where the ties should be placed.

Thread a large needle (one with a large eye, such as a tapestry needle) with yarn, $\frac{1}{16}$" ribbon, or string (button or quilting thread also works well). Working from the top of the quilt, push the needle through all layers, drawing the thread through, but not all the way. Leave a 6"–8" tail sticking out on top. About $\frac{1}{8}$"–$\frac{1}{4}$" from the first stitch, draw the needle back up (from the back to the front) through all layers. Cut the thread, again leaving a tail about 6"–8" long. Tie these two tails tightly together, using a double or triple knot to hold the tie se-

curely in place. You can make a bow with the excess, or simply trim the tails to about 1".

To Quilt by Machine

After the layers are securely pinned or basted, roll up to one-half of the quilt tightly enough to allow it to fit under the head of your sewing machine. You can safety-pin it closed or use bicycle clips to hold the roll. With larger quilts, you may need a friend to help guide the bulk through while you are quilting the center block.

Starting with the seams shown in Fig. 4-13, stitch "anchoring" quilt lines to hold all layers in place. This stitching will secure all layers of fabric and help keep the remainder of the quilt from shifting. It also helps to smooth the top and bottom toward you occasionally, with one hand above and one hand below, palms pressed gently together, and fingers spread.

After you have stitched the lines shown in Fig. 4-13, continue quilting by machine, following the outline of the pattern by sewing along the seam lines of the pieced quilt top. Be sure to back-tack the beginning and end of each quilting seam. I like to use thread that matches one of the lighter fabrics. When quilting along a seam that joins a solid color to a print fabric, try to keep your quilting stitches on the printed fabric, to the side of the seam.

Today's polyester fiberfills don't clump or shift as much as natural battings, like wool or cotton, because of the resins that hold the polyester fibers together. The stitching lines suggested here

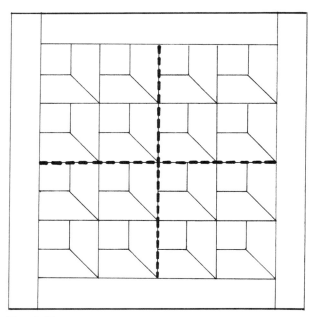

Fig. 4-13

are adequate to hold polyester fiberfill in place, but you may wish to add some extra quilting lines or ties if you are using pure wool or cotton batting.

Alternate Method of Finishing

1. Another method of finishing your quilt is to sew the face to the backing, right sides together, leaving the top edge open. Because these seams are so long, it helps to pin the edges together before sewing, to hold them in place. Be sure the back is cut to the exact size of the face before sewing them together.

2. Before turning right side out, lay your top and backing, which have been sewn together on three sides, right side down on a large, clean, flat surface. If you don't have a large enough floor space, lay it on as large a table as you can, with the open, unseamed end hanging over the edge of the table, and the bottom half of the quilt lying flat on the table. Place the polyester fiberfill on top and trim it to the exact size of the quilt.

3. Starting at the end opposite the opening, roll the entire quilt, like a sleeping bag, or jelly roll, until you have a long "tube" of fabric and batting (Fig. 4-14).

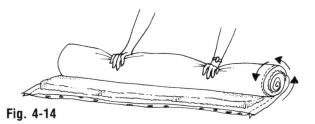

Fig. 4-14

4. Carefully reach inside the layers of fabric (between the face and backing), and slowly pull the tube inside-out, through the opening (Fig. 4-15).

Fig. 4-15

5. Slowly unwrap the quilt (Fig. 4-16), which will open, filled with fiberfill, and with three of the edges finished. (Practice with a sock. First, roll the sock, starting at the toe, and pull the cuff back over the roll. Slowly unroll it from the inside out, reaching inside the sock, between the layers, and pulling gently on the roll.)

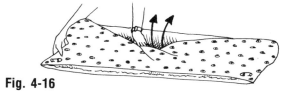

Fig. 4-16

6. Lay the quilt on a large, flat surface, and pin or baste through all layers. Hand or machine quilt, or tie it, as described above.

7. Turn the remaining edges to the inside, pin to hold, and machine stitch to close.

Make a Crib Quilt (44″ × 54″)

Materials Needed

Fabric

¾ yard each of two fabrics

1½ yards of the fabric that will also be used for the side strips

Batting and Backing

Polyester fiberfill: 44″ × 54″

Backing fabric: 1¾ yards of 44/45″ wide fabric

Don't Forget

Thread (for piecing your quilt face, as well as for hand or machine quilting, if desired)

String, yarn, or 1/16″ ribbon for tying your quilt, if you prefer

Graph paper or plain paper (which you have scored with 1″ squares) for pattern making

1. Make your pattern pieces in the dimensions given on the pattern guides on pages 4-15 and 4-16. See "Getting Started" and "Making the Pattern" in the instructions for the large quilts.

2. Before cutting the patchwork pieces, cut the side strips from the appropriate fabric. You will need two strips 7″ × 42″ and two strips 7″ × 45″.

3. Cut out your fabric patchwork pieces. Use Fig. 4-3 as a guide for cutting piece B and follow the instructions on the pattern guide.

4. Follow the instructions in "Sewing the Main Quilt Block" on page 4-4. You will piece 12 blocks, then sew them together with 4 blocks down and 3 across.

5. Sew the 7″ × 42″ strips to the *sides* of the finished quilt center. Sew the remaining strips to the top and bottom.

6. Refer to "Finishing the Quilt" from the instructions for the large quilt project to complete the crib quilt. The "Alternate Method of Finishing" is particularly easy when used on the crib quilt project.

Make a Wall Hanging (36″ square)

Materials Needed

Fabric

½ yard each of two fabrics

1¼ yards of the fabric that will also be used for the side strips

Batting and Backing

Polyester fiberfill: 36″ square

Backing fabric: 1¼ yards, cut to fit the face of the wall hanging

Don't Forget

Thread (for piecing your quilt face, as well as for hand or machine quilting, if desired)

String, yarn, or 1/16″ ribbon for tying your quilt, if you prefer

Graph paper or plain paper (which you have scored with 1″ squares) for pattern making

1. Make your pattern pieces in the dimensions given on the pattern guides on pages 4-15 and 4-16. See "Getting Started" and "Making the Pattern" in the instructions for the large quilts.

2. Before cutting the patchwork pattern pieces, cut the side strips from the appropriate farbic. You will need two strips 4″ × 32″ and two strips 4″ × 38″.

3. Cut out your fabric patchwork pieces. Use Fig. 4-3 as a guide for cutting piece B and follow the instructions on the pattern guide.

4. Follow the instructions in "Sewing the Main Quilt Block," on page 4-4, *except* you will piece nine blocks and sew them into three rows of three.

5. Sew the 4″ × 32″ strips to the *sides* of the finished quilt center. Sew the remaining strips to the top and bottom to complete the wall hanging face.

6. Refer to "Finishing the Quilt" from the instructions for the large quilt project to complete the wall hanging. The "Alternate Method of Finishing" is particularly easy when used on the wall hanging project.

You will probably want to make loops of fabric to sew to the top of the wall hanging or just behind the upper edge (hidden) to allow for a dowel rod to hang it.

To Make the Loops

For **hidden loops**, cut three pieces of fabric 1½" × 4". Fold the long edges inward to meet at the center, then fold the whole strip in half lengthwise. Using a straight stitch, sew through all layers along the "open" edge to make a small ribbon of fabric. Attach one in the middle of the upper edge of the wall hanging, and the remaining two at either side on the upper edge. Tack these to the wall hanging through all layers using your sewing machine, or hand sew them in place (Fig. 4-17).

For **decorative loops**, cut three pieces of matching fabric 3" × 5". Fold these in half, right sides together, to create 1½" × 5" pieces. Using a ⅜" seam allowance, sew a straight line down the 5" raw edge. Turn these tubes right side out and press so the seam is centered on one side. Fold these in half widthwise to hide the seam. Attach to the top of your wall hanging by machine, spacing the loops evenly.

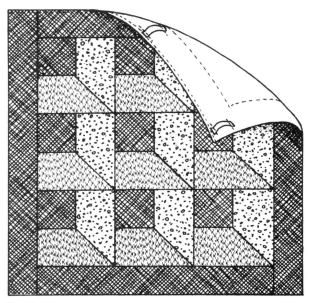

Fig. 4-17

For **bow loops**, cut three pieces of wide ribbon, each 24" long. Fold these in half and tack them to the top edge of your wall hanging by hand or machine, evenly spaced. Tie these loosely around a decorative pole or dowel rod.

The wall hanging is a perfect size for use as a table topper, lap quilt, or sofa throw.

Make a 16" Throw Pillow

Fabric Requirements

Face: ¼ yard each of three fabrics (Fabrics 1, 2, and 3)

Back: ½ yard of a matching fabric or a coordinating solid

Ruffle or cord: ⅝ yard

1. Make your pattern pieces in the dimensions given on the pattern guides on pages 4-15 and 4-16. See "Making the Pattern" in the instructions for the large quilts.

2. Cut out your fabric pieces according to the instructions on the pattern guides.

3. Follow the steps in "Sewing the Main Quilt Block" in the instructions for the large quilts. (You will not add side strips.) You will piece only four blocks, then sew them together to form a square.

4. You may quilt the pillow face before constructing the pillow if you wish (although this is not necessary). If you do, layer it with a backing and fiberfill cut to the same size as the face, then hand or machine quilt along the seams.

5. See the instructions on page 4-13 for making and applying ruffling and bias cording. With raw edges together, sew bias cording (Fig. 4-18) or a ruffle (Fig. 4-19) around the entire pillow face with a ⅜" seam allowance. You will need about 2 yards of bias cording or finished ruffling to go around the pillow. (This is sewn to the face side of the pillow.) For a knife-edge pillow, with no extra trim, you can eliminate this step.

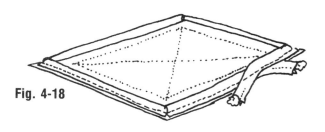

Fig. 4-18

Fig. 4-19

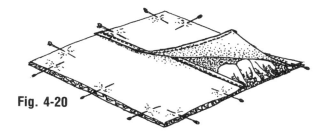

Fig. 4-20

6. Cut two pieces of backing fabric, 10″ × 17″. Finish one 17″ edge on each of these two pieces with a double-folded ¼″ hem, machine stitched.

7. Lay the pillow, right side up, with ruffle or cording toward the center. Place the backing right side down, on the pillow, overlapping the finished edges evenly in the center. Pin around the edges (Fig. 4-20).

8. Sew around the entire pillow, following the seam used to sew the cording or ruffle in place, or using a ⅜″ seam allowance. Turn inside out through the overlapped backing. Trim away any excess around the seams before turning.

9. Insert a 15″ or 16″ pillow form.

Make Your Own 15″–16″ Pillow Form

1. Save your scrap fiberfill.

2. Cut two 18″ squares of any white or ivory fabric.

3. Sew these together on three sides, using a ½″ seam allowance. Turn right side out.

4. Cut two 17″ squares of leftover fiberfill, and carefully slide them into the pillow cover. Con-tinue to stuff smaller bits of fiberfill between the squares, until the pillow is plump, but not too hard.

5. To finish, whipstitch the opening by hand. I call this a 15″–16″ finished size because the finished size will vary according to the plumpness of the pillow.

Make a Removable Chair Pad Cover

Note: An additional ⅓ yard of one of the fabrics is required for each chair pad.

1. Complete the 16″ pillow cover as explained above in "Make a 16″ Throw Pillow."

2. Cut two strips of fabric, 44″ × 5″. With a roll-hem attachment for your sewing machine, or a narrow double fold, hem around all sides of both strips (Fig. 4-21). Fold each in half, matching the two short ends, to create two tie ends, and pinch or pleat at the fold to gather. At what will be the back two corners, machine stitch the ties to the pillow cover, on the underside of the finished pillow, under the ruffle (Fig. 4-22).

3. To make a removable chair pad insert, pur-chase or make a 15″–16″ pillow form. With a long needle and double heavy-duty thread, run the thread through the center of the pillow form, leav-

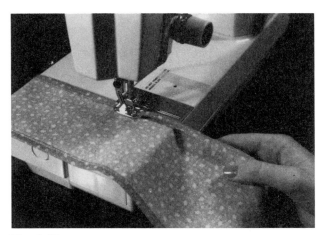

Fig. 4-21

Fig. 4-22

ing a "tail" of thread about 6″ long. Bring the needle back through about ½″ from the first stitch, and tie the ends of the thread, pulling tightly to form a "tuft" in the center.

Two matching chair pads with inserts make a lovely rocker set (Fig. 4-23).

Fig. 4-23

Make a Standard Pillow Sham

Fabric Requirements

Face: ¼ yard of one of three fabrics (Fabric 1, 2, or 3); ½ yard of the other two fabrics (includes side strips)
Back: ⅔ yard
Ruffle: ⅞ yard

1. Make your pattern pieces in the dimensions given on the pattern guides on pages 4-15 and 4-16. See "Making the Pattern" in the instructions for the large quilts.

2. Follow the piecing instructions for completing the 16″ throw pillow face.

3. Cut two strips 3½″ × 17″ of one of the fabrics and two strips 2″ × 23″ of the same fabric.

4. From another one of the fabrics cut two strips 3½″ × 21″ and two strips 2″ × 29″.

5. Add the 3½″ × 17″ strips to opposite sides of the quilt block, trimming away any excess. Add the 2″ × 23″ strips of the same fabric, in the same manner, to the remaining edges.

6. Add the 3½″ × 21″ strips of the other fabric to the first sides (as in Step 5), and add the remaining strips to the last two sides.

7. You may wish to first quilt the sham face. If so, layer it with a backing and fiberfill, cut to the same size as the face, then hand or machine quilt along the seams. This is not necessary, simply a matter of preference.

8. See the instructions on page 4-13 for making and applying bias cording and ruffling. With raw edges together, sew bias cording (Fig. 4-24) and/or

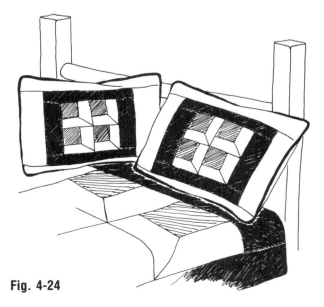

Fig. 4-24

fle around the entire sham face (see Figs. 4-18, 4-19). You will need about 3 yards of bias cording or finished ruffling to go around the pillow sham. (This is sewn to the right side of the pillow sham.)

9. Cut two pieces of a backing fabric, 16″ × 24″, finishing one 24″ edge on each piece with a narrow double-folded hem, machine stitched.

10. Lay the pillow sham right side up, with ruffle

pressed toward the center. Place the backing right side down, on the sham, overlapping the finished edges evenly in the center. Pin around the edges (see Fig. 4-20).

11. Sew around the entire pillow sham, following the seam used to sew ruffling and/or cording in place. Turn inside out through the overlapped backing. Trim away any excess around the seams before turning right-side out.

How to Make Matching Ruffling and Bias Cording for Pillows, Shams, and Chair Pads

Ruffling

You will need about ⅝ yard of extra fabric for ruffles around pillows and chair pads. You will need about ⅞ yard for pillow shams.

1. From the width of the fabric (44/45″) cut three 7″ strips (four for pillow shams), and sew them together on the short ends to make a long circle of fabric. Press the seam allowances open (Fig. 4-25).

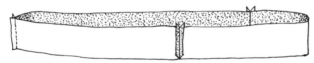

Fig. 4-25

2. Fold the circle in half lengthwise, so the raw edges meet, and right sides face out. Press.

3. With a wide basting stitch, sew about ¼″ from the raw edge (Fig. 4-26).

Fig. 4-26

4. Divide the circle equally into quarters, identifying the quarter marks with a straight pin. Pin the circle to the center of each straight edge on all four sides of your project, using the pins that mark the quarters to hold the ruffle in place.

5. Pull the basting stitch until the circle gathers into a ruffle equal to the size of the project you are working on. Use straight pins to hold the ruffle in place around the outer edge of the project, right sides together, as you gather it to fit (see Fig. 4-19).

Bias Cording

You will need ⅝ yard of matching fabric to make your own bias cording.

1. Cut 1½″-wide strips of fabric on the bias of the fabric. The strip of bias-cut fabric should be several inches longer than the measurement around the edge of the project you wish to trim.

2. Using purchased cording, wrap the bias strip around the cording so that wrong sides and raw edges meet. With a zipper foot attachment, stitch close to the cord, but not too snug, through both layers of fabric (Fig. 4-27).

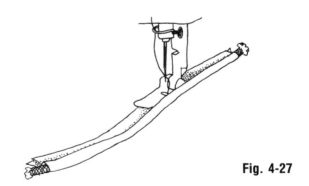

Fig. 4-27

3. The simplest application of the finished bias cording is to begin sewing it on one straight edge, keeping the raw edges of the bias tape and your project even, but with the starting end angled off the edge. Sew around the entire project, clipping the seam allowance of the bias tape at the corners. When you reach your starting point, overlap the bias tape, sewing over the angled end, and carefully angle the final end to sew it off the edge (see Fig. 4-18). Clip it to trim.

You may also apply bias tape by starting in the middle of one side, but start your seam about 2″ from the end of the bias tape. Sew all around as described above, but when you get to where you started, open the seam on the 2″ tail of the bias tape and pull back the fabric to show the cord. Clip off the 2″ of cord, and fold the fabric that is left in half, to create a 1″ tail (fold the fabric to the inside, so that only the right side shows). Cut the other end of the bias tape so it ends exactly where the first cord now starts. Wrap the folded bias tape fabric around this raw edge, and finish your seam.

Make a Placemat

Fabric Requirements

Face: ¼ yard each of three fabrics (Fabrics 1, 2, and 3)

Back: ½ yard of fabric will allow enough for *two* placemats.

1. Make your pattern pieces in the dimensions given on the pattern guides on pages 4-15 and 4-16.

2. Cut all fabric pieces according to the instructions.

3. Follow the piecing instructions for completing the 16″ throw pillow face.

4. Cut two strips of fabric, 2½″ × 17″, and sew them to opposite sides of the finished pillow face, trimming away any excess. Press all seams.

5. Cut a rectangle of backing fabric 17″ × 20″. Center this, right sides together, on the finished placemat face. Trim excess fabric from the placemat face to equal the size of the backing. Sew together with a ⅜″ seam allowance all around, except for a 4″ opening centered on one of the seams. Clip the corners and turn inside out through the opening. Hand or machine stitch the opening and press all around.

6. To minimize raveling or fraying of the seams on the inside when these are washed, you may wish to "quilt" along the seam lines, even though these do not have fiberfill. (You may add fiberfill, if you wish.)

Facets Pattern Guides

Dimensions include ⅜″ seam allowance

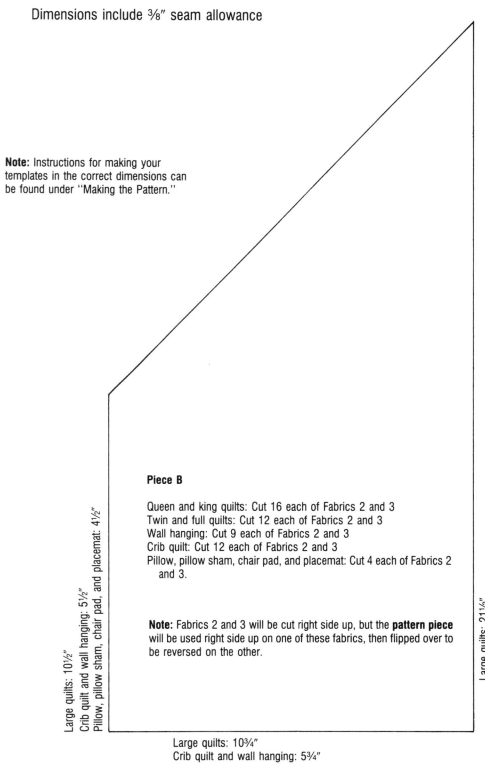

Note: Instructions for making your templates in the correct dimensions can be found under "Making the Pattern."

Piece B

Queen and king quilts: Cut 16 each of Fabrics 2 and 3
Twin and full quilts: Cut 12 each of Fabrics 2 and 3
Wall hanging: Cut 9 each of Fabrics 2 and 3
Crib quilt: Cut 12 each of Fabrics 2 and 3
Pillow, pillow sham, chair pad, and placemat: Cut 4 each of Fabrics 2 and 3.

Note: Fabrics 2 and 3 will be cut right side up, but the **pattern piece** will be used right side up on one of these fabrics, then flipped over to be reversed on the other.

Large quilts: 10½″
Crib quilt and wall hanging: 5½″
Pillow, pillow sham, chair pad, and placemat: 4½″

Large quilts: 21½″
Crib quilt and wall hanging: 11½″
Pillow, pillow sham, chair pad, and placemat: 9¾″

Large quilts: 10¾″
Crib quilt and wall hanging: 5¾″
Pillow, pillow sham, chair pad, and placemat: 4¾″

Piece A

Queen and king quilts: Cut 16 of Fabric 1, 10¾″ square
Twin and full quilts: Cut 12 of Fabric 1, 10¾″ square
Crib quilt: Cut 12 of Fabric 1, 5¾″ square
Wall hanging: Cut 9 of Fabric 1, 5¾″ square
Pillow, pillow sham, chair pad, and placemat: Cut 4 of Fabric 1, 4¾″

SUPER SIMPLE QUILTS #5
WILD GOOSE CHASE

Make a Quilt

In this section you will find all the information you need to make a twin, full, queen, or king-size quilt. Instructions for making a crib-size quilt or wall hanging begin on page 5-9.

Getting Started

Wild Goose Chase is composed of rows of large triangles set off by contrasting small triangles and strips of fabric. You can use a variety of different fabrics for this quilt project, which can actually be more interesting when made with five or six different colors. You can make it in prints or solid-color fabrics, or both. When using prints, I recommend that you avoid stripes, plaids, or checks, and that you be consistent in the size of the print (for example, use all large florals or all small calicoes). Finally, if you use a print, use it in either the large triangles or the small—not both. The success of this pattern comes from the fabric you use in the small triangles. For best results, use one coordinating solid-color fabric in all of the small triangles to frame or offset the larger ones.

The instructions here are for three colors. "Fabric 1" is for the large triangles and one outer border. (The large triangles can also be done in assorted fabrics. Because of the size of the pattern, you'll need at least ⅜ of a yard for each large triangle. If the fabric doesn't have a one-way design, you can get two large triangles from ⅜ yard.) "Fabric 2" is for the smaller triangles. "Fabric 3" is for the sashing strip and narrow border that frames the center quilt block.

Materials Needed

Fabric

Yardage amounts listed below are approximate and will allow for some leftover fabric— enough to make several pillows, or two pillow shams, or a wall hanging or baby quilt. Yardages for backing are given in the following section.

Batting and Backing

Polyester fiberfill or wool or cotton batting large enough to complete your quilt.

A large, flat sheet or extra-wide fabric, large enough to use as a backing on your quilt. Three yards of 108″ sheeting (available at well-supplied fabric stores) will fit all sizes. Or you can use 44/45″ wide fabric as follows: For twin and full sizes, you need 5½ yards of 44/45″ wide fabric, cut in two pieces, each 2¾ yards long. Seam them together along the selvages (Fig. 5-1). For queen and king sizes, you need 8¼ yards of 44/45″ wide fabric, cut in three pieces, each 2¾ yards, seamed together along the selvages (Fig. 5-2).

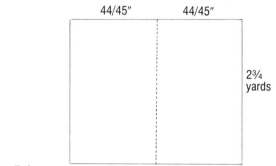

Fig. 5-1 Back for twin or full

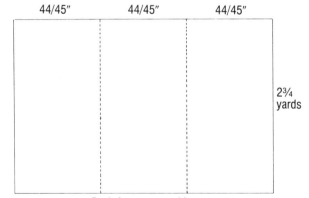

Fig. 5-2 Back for queen or king

	Fabric 1	Fabric 2	Fabric 3
Twin (90″ × 68″)	3 yards	3 yards	1⅔ yards
Full (90″ × 76″)	4 yards	3¾ yards	1⅔ yards
Queen (90″ × 90″)	4½ yards	4 yards	1⅔ yards
King (90″ × 102″)	5 yards	4½ yards	1⅔ yards

When laying out the backing, batting, and quilt top in preparation for quilting, center the quilt top so the seams in the back are equal distances from the sides.

Don't Forget

Thread (for piecing your quilt face, as well as for hand or machine quilting, if desired)

String, yarn, or 1/16" ribbon for tying your quilt, if you prefer

Graph paper or plain paper (which you have scored with 1" squares) for pattern making

Making the Pattern

Making the pattern is as easy as counting squares and connecting dots. The pattern guides at the end of this project give dimensions for making your own pattern pieces. You may use graph paper, gridded freezer paper, or tracing paper taped to a 1" gridded cutting board. Graph paper is available in a variety of "squares-to-the-inch" sizes. It doesn't matter what size you choose, as long as the 1" lines are clearly visible. If you are using smaller pieces of graph paper, carefully tape them together using clear tape, making sure the lines match up vertically and horizontally.

Start by marking a dot on the corner of one square on the grid. This represents one corner of your pattern. Using the 1" grid on your paper, count, either straight up or down, or sideways, exactly the number of inches (squares) indicated on the pattern guide at the end of this project. It helps to have an extra ruler on hand to add a fraction of an inch where needed. Mark another dot when you have reached the number of squares

you want, and draw a line between the dots. Continue in this manner until the pattern piece is complete.

Before drawing your angled lines, first draw the straight horizontal and vertical lines. Then just connect the ends of these lines to create the angled line to complete your pattern piece.

Do not add seam allowances! Unlike in some quilt pattern books, these patterns already include a 3/8" seam allowance.

After you have drawn your pattern pieces on the grid, double-check all measurements, then carefully cut them out (Fig. 5-3).

Fig. 5-3

Cutting the Fabric

Rotary cutting tools are ideal for cutting your strips and pattern pieces. Before cutting the patchwork pattern pieces, cut the side strips as follows:

Bed size	Fabric 1	Fabric 2
Twin	2 each, 11" × 66" 2 each, 5" × 98"	2 each, 11" × 56" 2 each, 5" × 78"
Full	2 each, 11" × 74" 2 each, 8" × 98"	2 each, 11" × 56" 2 each, 8" × 78"
Queen	2 each, 11" × 78" 2 each, 10" × 98"	2 each, 11" × 56" 2 each, 10" × 78"
King	2 each, 11" × 84" 2 each, 14" × 98"	2 each, 11" × 56" 2 each, 14" × 78"

You also need to cut the following strips of Fabric 3 for *all* sizes:

1 strip 4″ × 48″ (center)
2 strips 5″ × 48″ (top and bottom)
2 strips 4″ × 56″ (sides)

These strips of Fabric 3 will be used to complete the quilt center.

Note: The center pattern of the quilt is the same for all four bed sizes. The variation in quilt size comes from the different sizes of side strips added after the quilt center is pieced. The strip sizes shown above are generous, to allow for slight variations in seam allowances or stretch of the fabric. You may trim away the excess after the strip is sewn in place.

After you have cut your strips, cut the patchwork pattern pieces. The number of pieces needed is shown on the pattern guides on page 5-16.

Sewing the Main Quilt Block

Hint #1: When one or both pattern pieces is being sewn on a bias (angle-cut) edge, it helps to pin the edges together to prevent pulling or stretching the fabric. Otherwise, it is not necessary to pin pieces together before sewing them. In fact, it's quicker and easier not to. Just be sure you're letting the machine do the work, and that you're not pulling, or "force-guiding," the fabric, which causes bias-cut fabrics to stretch or distort. You can also eliminate this potential problem by using a walking foot on your sewing machine.

Hint #2: Don't worry if your edges don't match perfectly when you are sewing them together. The seams are hidden inside the quilt. And the quilting stitches or ties help camouflage minor flaws. It's the total finished look that will make you proud to give or display your handiwork.

Hint #3: As you work, press all seam allowances toward the darker of the fabrics to prevent seam allowances from being noticeable through lighter-colored fabrics.

1. After cutting out all pattern pieces, lay one small triangle on the large triangle as shown (Fig. 5-4), and sew using a ⅜″ seam allowance. Now sew the other small triangle to the same large triangle. The short sides of the large triangle should line up with the longest side of the small triangles when laid face-to-face for seaming. You will end up with a large rectangle (Fig. 5-5).

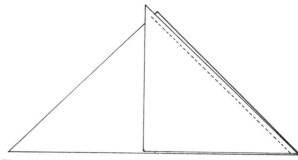

Fig. 5-4

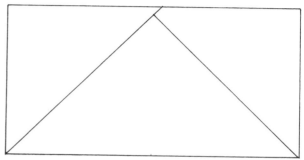

Fig. 5-5

2. Continue to piece these rectangles, until all eight are complete. Then sew them together in two vertical rows of four.

3. Now take the 4″ × 48″ sashing strip of Fabric 3 and sew it between these two rows with ⅜″ seam allowances (Fig. 5-6). Some extra length has been allowed in the strips of Fabric 3. Trim any excess

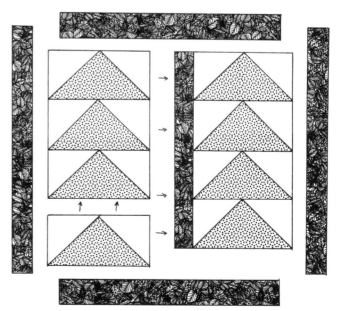

Fig. 5-6

after the strip is sewn in place. Sew the 5″ × 48″ strips of Fabric 3 to the top and bottom of this piece, then sew the 4″ × 56″ strips of Fabric 3 to the sides, to complete the center block. Press all seams.

Sewing on the Side Strips

1. Sew the shorter strips of Fabric 2 to the top and bottom edges of the quilt center with a ⅜″ seam allowance. Trim any excess.

2. Sew the longer strips of Fabric 2 to the two opposite edges, including in the seam the strips that were already added (creating a large rectangle). Trim excess.

3. Sew the shorter strips of Fabric 1 to the top and bottom. Trim excess.

4. Finally, sew the remaining longest strips of Fabric 1 to the last two sides of the quilt to complete the face (Fig. 5-7). Trim excess. Press all seams toward dark.

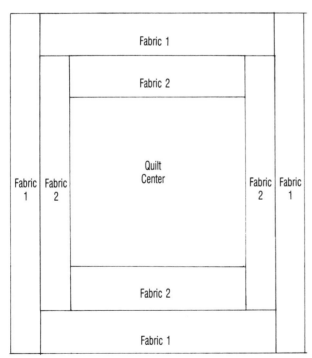

Fig. 5-7

Finishing the Quilt

1. Cut and seam the backing fabric, if necessary, to equal the size of your finished quilt top (see page 5-3).

2. Lay the backing (sheet, sheeting, or seamed fabric) right side down on a large, clean surface.

3. Place the polyester fiberfill or other batting on top of the backing.

4. Lay the quilt top right side up on the fiberfill. Hand baste, or pin using large safety pins, through all layers to hold them in place. (I prefer safety pins to straight pins because they save my hands and other body parts from pinpricks as I work.)

5. Using yarn, string, or 1/16″ ribbon, tie the layers firmly, or quilt the layers by hand or machine, as desired. Instructions follow.

6. Finish the edges, using bias tape or other decorative trim, as desired (Fig. 5-8). The edges can also be turned easily to the inside and sewn in place by machine (Fig. 5-9). You can insert piping, lace, or a ruffle at the edge with this method.

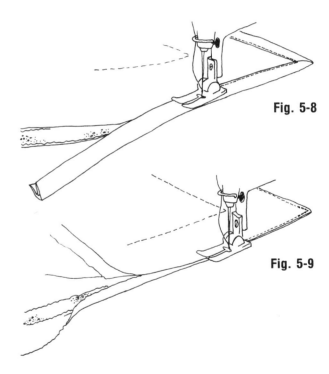

Fig. 5-8

Fig. 5-9

To Add Bias Tape

There are many ways to apply a bias taped edge, but in general, it is easiest if you sew a seam around your entire project, using a narrow seam allowance, to keep the layers from stretching or shifting *before* you apply the bias tape.

Starting in the middle of one side of your project, and using long straight pins, pin the bias tape around the entire piece, overlapping and folding under the last edge where it meets with your starting point. When you get to a corner, tuck the excess flatly and neatly inside of itself, by gently pushing it to one side with pointed scissors or a pin. It may help to open the bias tape so it is flat when you get to a corner, then pinch the excess to guide it into the fold at the corner (Fig. 5-10). Hand baste or topstitch by machine over the miter.

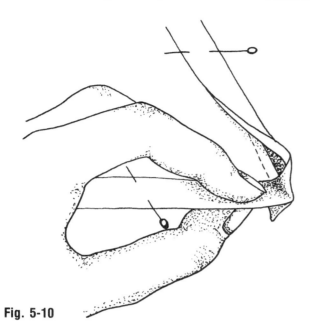

Fig. 5-10

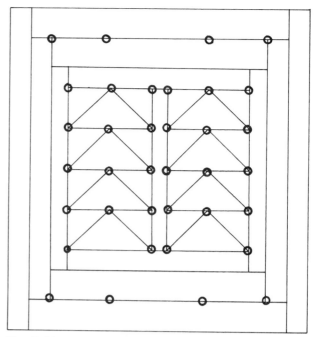

Fig. 5-11

There are a number of quilt books available with chapters devoted to finishing the edges of your quilt. Some books have been written solely on the subject. Your local library or bookstore should have a variety of books to choose from.

To Tie Your Quilt

Tying your quilt is the easiest way to hold the layers together and provides a quick finish to your quilt. Baste or pin the layers of your quilt to hold them in place before you begin. It is not necessary to mark the points at which you will tie your quilt. Figure 5-11 shows where the ties should be placed.

Thread a large needle (one with a large eye, such as a tapestry needle) with yarn, $1/16''$ ribbon, or string (button or quilting thread also works well). Working from the top of the quilt, push the needle through all layers, drawing the thread through, but not all the way. Leave a 6"–8" tail sticking out on top. About $1/8''$–$1/4''$ from the first stitch, draw the needle back up (from the back to the front) through all layers. Cut the thread, again leaving a tail about 6"–8" long. Tie these two tails tightly together, using a double or triple knot to hold the tie securely in place. You can make a bow with the excess, or simply trim the tails to about 1".

To Quilt by Machine

After the layers are securely pinned or basted, roll up to one-half of the quilt tightly enough to allow it to fit under the head of your sewing machine. You can safety-pin it closed or use bicycle clips to hold the roll. With larger quilts, you may need a friend to help guide the bulk through while you are quilting the center block.

Starting with the seams shown in Fig. 5-12, stitch "anchoring" quilt lines to hold all layers in place. This stitching will secure all layers of fabric and help keep the remainder of the quilt from shifting. It also helps to smooth the top and bottom toward you occasionally, with one hand above and one hand below, palms pressed gently together, and fingers spread (Fig 5-13).

After you have stitched the lines shown in Fig. 5-12, continue quilting by machine, following the outline of the pattern by sewing along the seam lines of the pieced quilt top. Be sure to back-tack the beginning and end of each quilting seam. I like to use thread that matches one of the lighter fabrics. When quilting along a seam that joins a solid color to a print fabric, try to keep your quilting stitches on the printed fabric, to the side of the seam.

Today's polyester fiberfills don't clump or shift as much as natural battings, like wool or cotton, because of the resins that hold the polyester fibers together. The stitching lines suggested here are adequate to hold polyester fiberfill in place,

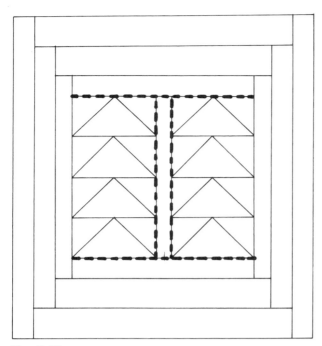

Fig. 5-12

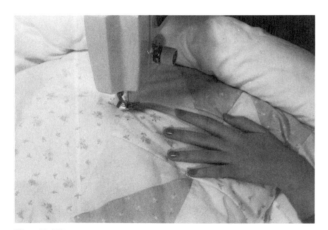

Fig. 5-13

but you may wish to add some extra quilting lines or ties if you are using pure wool or cotton batting.

Alternate Method of Finishing

1. Another method of finishing your quilt is to sew the face to the backing, right sides together, leaving the top edge open. Because these seams are so long, it helps to pin the edges together before sewing, to hold them in place. Be sure the back is cut to the exact size of the face before sewing them together.

2. Before turning right side out, lay your top and backing, which have been sewn together on three sides, right side down on a large, clean, flat surface. If you don't have a large enough floor space, lay it on as large a table as you can, with the open, unseamed end hanging over the edge of the table, and the bottom half of the quilt lying flat on the table. Place the polyester fiberfill on top and trim it to the exact size of the quilt.

3. Starting at the end opposite the opening, roll the entire quilt, like a sleeping bag, or jelly roll, until you have a long "tube" of fabric and batting (Fig. 5-14).

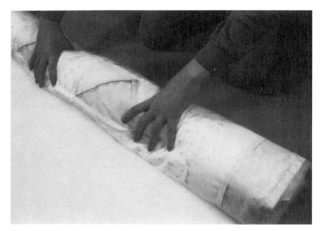

Fig. 5-14

4. Carefully reach inside the layers of fabric (between the face and backing), and slowly pull the tube inside-out, through the opening (Fig. 5-15).

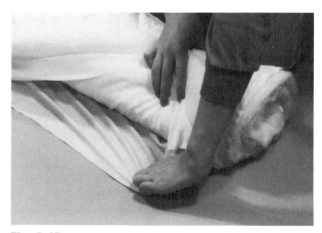

Fig. 5-15

5. Slowly unwrap the quilt, which will open, filled with fiberfill, and three of the edges finished (Fig. 5-16). (Practice with a sock. First, roll the sock, starting at the toe, and pull the cuff back over the roll. Slowly unroll it from the inside out, reaching inside the sock, between the layers, and pulling gently on the roll.)

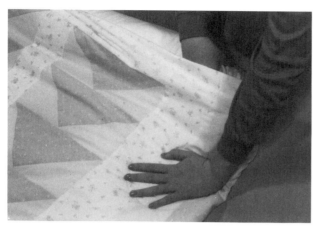

Fig. 5-16

6. Lay the quilt on a large, flat surface, and pin or baste through all layers. Hand or machine quilt, or tie it, as described above.

7. Turn the remaining edges to the inside, pin to hold, and machine stitch to close.

Make a Crib Quilt (42″ × 52″)

Materials Needed

Fabric

Fabric 1: 1¾ yards
Fabric 2: 1⅓ yards
Fabric 3: ½ yard

Batting and Backing

Polyester fiberfill: 44″ × 54″
Backing fabric: 1¾ yards of 44/45″ wide fabric

Don't Forget

Thread (for piecing your quilt face, as well as for hand or machine quilting, if desired)
String, yarn, or ¹⁄₁₆″ ribbon for tying your quilt, if you prefer
Graph paper or plain paper (which you have scored with 1″ squares) for pattern making

1. Make your pattern pieces in the dimensions given on the pattern guides on page 5-16. See "Getting Started" and "Making the Pattern" in the instructions for the large quilts.

2. Before cutting the patchwork pieces, cut strips as follows: From Fabric 1 cut two strips 7″ × 38″ and two strips 4″ × 56″. From Fabric 2 cut two strips 7″ × 30″ and two strips 4″ × 44″. From Fabric 3 cut one strip 4″ × 22″, two strips 6″ × 25″, and two strips 5″ × 32″. The Fabric 3 strips will be used to complete the quilt center. The other strips are the side strips.

3. Cut out your fabric patchwork pieces. The number needed is shown on the pattern guides on page 5-16.

4. Follow the instructions for the large quilt for sewing the triangles into rectangles (Figs. 5-4, 5-5), and these rectangles into strips. You will complete eight rectangles, or two vertical rows of four rectangles, as shown for the large quilt project (Fig. 5-6).

5. Sew the 4″ × 22″ strip of Fabric 3 between the two strips of rectangles, trimming away any excess from the strip of Fabric 3 (Fig. 5-6). Next sew the 6″ × 25″ strips of Fabric 3 to the top and bottom of the center block, again trimming any excess. Finally, sew the 5″ × 32″ strips to the sides to complete the center quilt block.

6. Follow the instructions in "Sewing on the Side Strips" and "Finishing the Quilt" beginning on page 5-6 to complete the crib quilt. (This pattern is simply a miniature version of the large quilt). The "Alternate Method of Finishing" is particularly nice when used on the crib quilt.

Make a Wall Hanging (36″ square)

Materials Needed

Fabric

Fabric 1, 1¼ yards
Fabric 2, 1 yard
Fabric 3, ½ yard

Batting and Backing

Backing fabric: 1¼ yards, cut to fit face of wall hanging
Batting: 38″ square

Don't Forget

Thread (for piecing your quilt face, as well as for hand or machine quilting, if desired)
String, yarn, or 1/16″ ribbon for tying your quilt, if you prefer
Graph paper or plain paper (which you have scored with 1″ squares) for pattern making

1. Make your pattern pieces in the dimensions given in the pattern guides on page 5-16. See "Getting Started" and "Making the Pattern" in the instructions for the large quilts.

2. Before cutting the patchwork pattern pieces, cut strips as follows: From Fabric 1 cut two strips 3″ × 35″ and two strips 3″ × 40″. From Fabric 2 cut two strips 3″ × 30″ and two strips 3″ × 35″. From Fabric 3 cut one strip 4″ × 22″, two strips 6″ × 25″, and two strips 5″ × 32″. (The Fabric 3 strips will be used to complete the quilt center; the other strips are side strips.)

3. Cut out your fabric patchwork pieces according to the instructions on the pattern on page 5-16.

4. Follow the instructions for the large quilts for sewing the triangles into rectangles (Figs. 5-4, 5-5), and these rectangles into strips. You will complete eight rectangles, or two vertical rows of four rectangles, as shown for the large quilt project.

5. Sew the 4″ × 22″ strip of Fabric 3 between the two strips of rectangles, trimming away any excess from the strip of Fabric 3 (Fig. 5-6). Next, sew the 6″ × 25″ strips of Fabric 3 to the top and bottom of the center block, again trimming any excess. Finally, sew the 5″ × 32″ strips to the sides to complete the center quilt block.

6. Follow the instructions from the large quilt project in "Sewing on the Side Strips" and "Finishing the Quilt" beginning on page 5-6 to complete the wall hanging. (This pattern is simply a miniature version of the large quilt.) The "Alternate Method of Finishing" is particularly nice when used on the wall hanging.

You will probably want to make loops of fabric to sew to the top of the wall hanging or just behind the upper edge (hidden) to allow for a dowel rod to hang it.

To Make the Loops

For **hidden loops**, cut three pieces of fabric 1½″ × 4″. Fold the long edges inward to meet at the center, then fold the whole strip in half lengthwise. Using a straight stitch, sew through all layers along the "open" edge to make a small "ribbon" of fabric. Attach one in the middle of the upper edge of the wall hanging, and the remaining two at either side on the upper edge. Tack these to the wall hanging through all layers using your sewing machine, or hand sew them in place.

For **decorative loops**, cut three pieces of matching fabric 3″ × 5″. Fold these in half, right sides together, to create 1½″ × 5″ pieces. Using a ⅜″ seam allowance, sew a straight line down the 5″

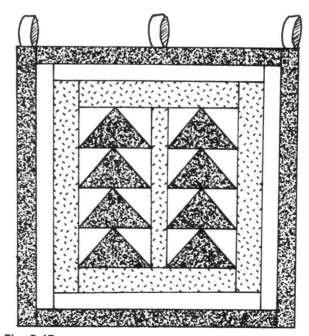

Fig. 5-17

raw edge. Turn these tubes right side out and press so the seam is centered on one side. Fold these in half widthwise to hide the seam. Attach to the top of your wall hanging by machine, spacing the loops evenly (Fig. 5-17).

For **bow loops**, cut three pieces of wide rib-bon, each 24″ long. Fold these in half and tack them to the top edge of your wall hanging by hand or machine, evenly spaced. Tie these loosely around a decorative pole or dowel rod.

The wall hanging is a perfect size for use as a table topper, lap quilt, or sofa throw.

Make a 16″ Throw Pillow

Fabric Requirements

Face: Use the scraps from the large quilt or ¼ yard each of three fabrics

Back: ½ yard of a matching fabric or a coordinating solid

Ruffle or cord: ⅝ yard

1. Make your pattern pieces in the dimensions given on the pattern guides on page 5-16. See "Getting Started" and "Making the Pattern" in the instructions for the large quilts.

2. Cut out your fabric pieces according to the instructions on the pattern guides.

3. Follow Step 1 (Figs. 5-4, 5-5) under "Sewing the Main Quilt Block" in the instructions for the large quilts. You will piece only two rectangles (Fig. 5-18). Press all seams.

4. From Fabric 3, cut two strips 3½″ × 12″, and sew these to the top and bottom of the pillow center. In the same way, cut two strips 3½″ × 18″ from Fabric 3, and sew these to the sides of the pillow (Fig. 5-18). Remember to use ⅜″ seam al-

lowances. Trim excess from the ends of the strips, as necessary. Press these seams.

5. You may wish to quilt the pillow face before constructing the pillow (although this is not necessary). If so, layer it with a plain muslin backing and fiberfill, cut to the same size as the face, then hand or machine quilt along the seams.

6. See the instructions on page 5-14 for making and applying ruffling and bias cording. With raw edges together, sew bias cording (Fig. 5-19) or a ruffle (Fig. 5-20) around the entire pillow face with a ⅜″ seam allowance. You will need about 2 yards of bias cording or finished ruffling to go around the pillow. (This is sewn to the face side of the pillow.) For a knife-edge pillow, with no extra trim, you can eliminate this step.

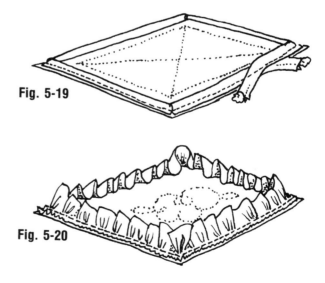

Fig. 5-19

Fig. 5-20

7. Cut two pieces of a backing fabric, 10″ × 17″. Finish one 17″ edge on each of these two pieces with a double-folded hem, machine stitched.

8. Lay the pillow, right side up, with ruffle or cording toward the center. Place the backing right side down, on the pillow, overlapping the finished edges evenly in the center. Pin around the edges (Fig. 5-21).

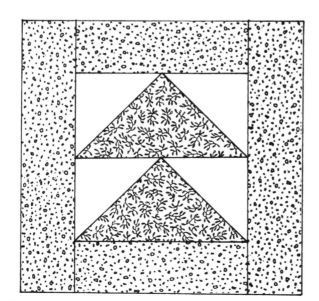

Fig. 5-18

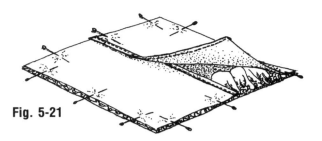

Fig. 5-21

9. Sew around the entire pillow, following the seam used to sew the cording or ruffle in place, or using a ⅜″ seam allowance. Turn inside out through the overlapped backing. Trim away any excess around the seams before turning.

10. Insert a 15″ or 16″ pillow form.

Make Your Own 15″–16″ Pillow Form

1. Save your scrap fiberfill.

2. Cut two 18″ squares of any white or ivory fabric.

3. Sew these together on three sides, using a ½″ seam allowance. Turn right side out.

4. Cut two 17″ squares of leftover fiberfill, and carefully slide them into the pillow cover. Con-

tinue to stuff smaller bits of fiberfill between the squares, until the pillow is plump, but not too hard.

5. To finish, whipstitch the opening by hand. I call this a 15″–16″ finished size because the finished size will vary according to the plumpness of the pillow.

Make a Removable Chair Pad Cover

Note: An additional ⅓ yard of one of the fabrics is required for each chair pad.

1. Complete the 16″ pillow cover as explained in "Make a 16″ Throw Pillow."

2. Cut two strips of fabric, 44″ × 5″. With a roll-hem attachment for your sewing machine, or a narrow double fold, hem around all sides of both strips (Fig. 5-22). Fold each in half, matching the two short ends, to create two tie ends, and pinch or pleat at the fold to gather (Fig. 5-23). At what will be the back two corners, machine stitch the ties to the pillow cover, on the underside of the finished pillow, under the ruffle (Fig. 5-24).

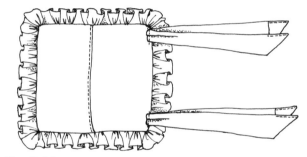

Fig. 5-24

3. To make a removable chair pad insert, purchase or make a 15″–16″ pillow form. With a long needle and double heavy-duty thread, run the thread through the center of the pillow form, leaving a "tail" of thread about 6″ long. Bring the needle back through about ½″ from the first stitch, and tie the ends of the thread, pulling tightly to form a "tuft" in the center.

Two matching chair pads with inserts make a lovely rocker set.

Fig. 5-22

Fig. 5-23

Make a Standard Pillow Sham

Fabric Requirements

Face: Use the scraps from the large quilt or ¼ yard of one of your three fabrics and ½ yard of the other two (to include side strips)

Back: ⅔ yard

Ruffle: ⅞ yard

1. Make your pattern pieces in the dimensions given on the pattern guides on page 5-16. See "Getting Started" and "Making the Pattern" in the instructions for the large quilts.

2. Cut out your fabric pieces. The number of pieces needed is given on the pattern guides.

3. Follow Steps 3 and 4 in the piecing instructions for completing the face of the 16″ throw pillow, including the strips of Fabric 3, to make a 17″ square.

4. Cut two strips of Fabric 2, 3½″ × 17″, and two strips 2″ × 23″.

5. Cut two strips of Fabric 1, 3½″ × 21″, and two strips 2″ × 29″.

6. Add the 3½″ × 17″ strips of Fabric 2 to opposite sides of the quilt block, trimming away any excess. Add the 2″ × 23″ strips of the same fabric, in the same manner, to the remaining edges.

7. Add the 3½″ × 21″ strips of Fabric 1 to the first sides (as in Step 5), and add the remaining strips to the last two sides.

8. You may wish to first quilt the sham face. If so layer it with a plain muslin backing and fiberfill cut to the same size as the face, then hand or machine quilt along the seams. This is not necessary, simply a matter of preference.

9. See the instructions on page 5-14 for making and applying bias cording and ruffling. With raw edges together, sew bias cording and/or a ruffle around the entire sham face (see Figs. 5-19 and 5-20). You will need about 3 yards of bias cording or finished ruffling to go around the pillow sham. (This is sewn to the right side of the pillow sham.)

10. Cut two pieces of a backing fabric, 16″ × 24″, finishing one 24″ edge on each piece with a narrow, double-folded hem, machine stitched.

11. Lay the pillow sham face up, with ruffle or bias cording pressed toward the center. Place the backing, right side down on the sham, overlapping the finished edges evenly in the center. Pin around the edges (see Fig. 5-21).

12. Sew around the entire pillow sham, following the seam used to sew ruffling and/or cording in place. Turn inside out through the overlapped backing. Trim away any excess around the seams before turning right-side out (Fig. 5-25, 5-26).

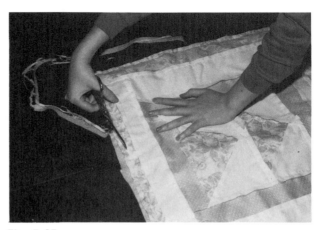

Fig. 5-25

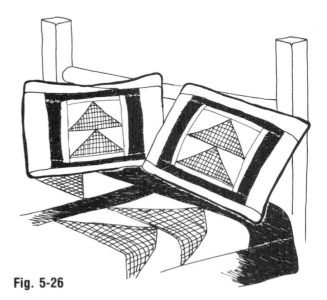

Fig. 5-26

How to Make Matching Ruffling and Bias Cording for Pillows, Shams, and Chair Pads

Ruffling

You will need about ⅝ yard of extra fabric for ruffles around pillows and chair pads. You will need about ⅞ yard for pillow shams.

1. From the width of the fabric (44/45″) cut three 7″ strips (four strips for pillow shams), and sew them together on the short ends to make a long circle of fabric. Press the seam allowances open (Fig. 5-27).

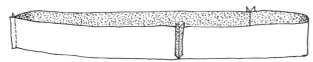

Fig. 5-27

2. Fold the circle in half lengthwise, so the raw edges meet, and right sides face out. Press.

3. With a wide basting stitch, sew about ¼″ from the raw edge (Fig. 5-28).

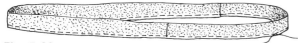

Fig. 5-28

4. Divide the circle equally into quarters, identifying the quarter marks with a straight pin. Pin the circle to the center of each straight edge on all four sides of your project, using the pins that mark the quarters to hold the ruffle in place.

5. Pull the basting stitch until the circle gathers evenly into a ruffle equal to the size of the project that you are working on. Use straight pins to hold the ruffle in place around the outer edge of the project, right sides together, as you gather it to fit (see Fig. 5-20).

Bias Cording

You will need ⅝ yard of matching fabric to make your own bias cording.

1. Cut a 1½″-wide strip of fabric on the bias. The strip of bias-cut fabric should be several inches longer than the measurement around the edge of the project you wish to trim.

2. Using purchased cording, wrap the bias tape around the cording so that raw edges meet. With a zipper foot attachment, stitch close to the cord, but not too snug, through both layers of fabric (Fig. 5-29).

3. The simplest application of the finished bias cording is to begin sewing it on one straight edge, keeping the raw edges of the bias tape and your project even, but with the starting end angled off the edge. Sew around the entire project, clipping the seam allowance of the bias tape at the corners. When you reach your starting point, overlap the bias tape, sewing over the angled end, and carefully angle the final end to sew it off the edge (see Fig. 5-19). Clip it to trim.

You may also apply bias tape by starting in the middle of one side, but start your seam about 2″ from the end of the bias tape. Sew all around as described above, but when you get to where you started, open the seam on the 2″ tail of the bias tape and pull back the fabric to show the cord. Clip off the 2″ of cord, and fold the fabric that is left in half, to create a 1″ tail (fold the fabric to the inside, so that only the right side shows). Cut the other end of the bias tape so it ends exactly where the first cord now starts. Wrap the folded bias tape fabric around this raw edge, and finish your seam.

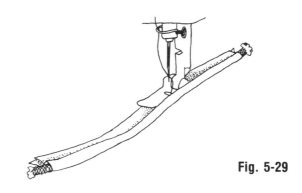

Fig. 5-29

Make a Placemat

Fabric Requirements

Face: Use the scrap from the large quilt or ¼ yard of each of your three fabrics

Back: ½ yard of fabric will allow enough for *two* placemats.

1. Make your pattern pieces in the dimensions given on the pattern guides on page 5-16. See "Getting Started" and "Making the Pattern" in the instructions for the large quilts.

2. Cut the pieces required as shown on the pattern guides on page 5-16.

3. Follow Step 1 (Figs. 5-4, 5-5) under "Sewing the Main Quilt Block" in the instructions for the large quilts. You will piece only two rectangles.

4. Cut two strips of Fabric 3, 5″ × 12″, and sew them to opposite sides of the center block. Trim any excess from the end of the strips. Cut two more strips of Fabric 3, 3½″ × 18″, and sew them to the remaining sides of the placemat. Trim any excess, and press all seams (see Fig. 5-18).

5. From Fabric 1, cut two strips 2½″ × 17″ and sew these to the sides of the finished square.

6. Cut a rectangle of backing fabric 17″ × 20″. Center this, right sides together, on the finished placemat face. Trim excess fabric from the placemat face to equal the size of the backing. Sew together with a ⅜″ seam allowance all around, except for a 4″ opening centered on one of the seams. Clip the corners and turn inside out through the opening. Hand or machine stitch the opening and press all around.

7. To minimize raveling or fraying of the seams on the inside when these are washed, you may wish to "quilt" along the seam lines, even though these do not have fiberfill. (You may add fiberfill, if you wish.)

Wild Goose Chase Pattern Guides

Dimensions include ⅜″ seam allowance.

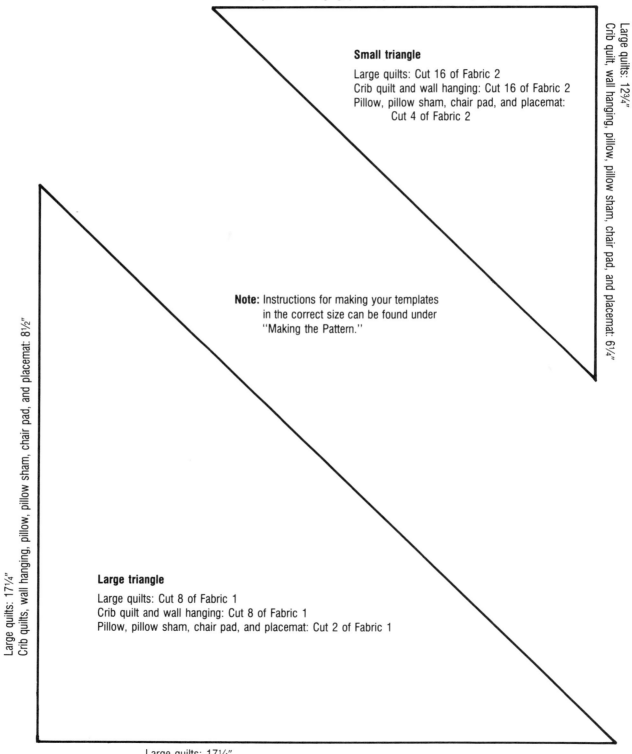

Large quilts: 12¾″
Crib quilt, wall hanging, pillow, pillow sham, chair pad, and placemat: 6¼″

Large quilts: 12¾″
Crib quilt, wall hanging, pillow, pillow sham, chair pad, and placemat: 6¼″

Small triangle

Large quilts: Cut 16 of Fabric 2
Crib quilt and wall hanging: Cut 16 of Fabric 2
Pillow, pillow sham, chair pad, and placemat:
  Cut 4 of Fabric 2

Note: Instructions for making your templates
in the correct size can be found under
"Making the Pattern."

Large quilts: 17¼″
Crib quilts, wall hanging, pillow, pillow sham, chair pad, and placemat: 8½″

Large triangle

Large quilts: Cut 8 of Fabric 1
Crib quilt and wall hanging: Cut 8 of Fabric 1
Pillow, pillow sham, chair pad, and placemat: Cut 2 of Fabric 1

Large quilts: 17¼″
Crib quilt, wall hanging, pillow, pillow sham, chair pad, and placemat: 8½″

SUPER SIMPLE QUILTS #6

OPTIKA

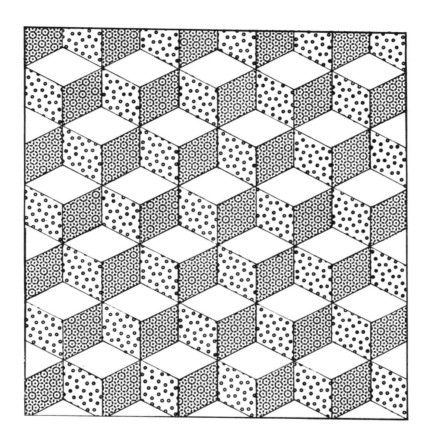

Make a Quilt

In this section you will find all the information you need to make a twin, full, queen, or king-size quilt. Instructions for making a crib-size quilt or wall hanging begin on page 6-9.

Getting Started

Optika, also known as Tumbling Blocks, creates an optical illusion with its shading of the three main pieces. Although Optika is one of the more difficult and intriguing of the Amish patterns, I have enlarged the pattern to simplify it and give it a more contemporary look. For best results, use starkly contrasting light- and dark-colored solid fabrics, with a medium shade or a blend of the dark and light colors, as the third fabric. (For example, try black, white, and gray.) Also dynamic, and great for children's rooms, are royal blue, flame red, and sunshine yellow. The crib quilt is a welcome gift in powder blue, petal pink, and pale yellow. Avoid fabrics with a nap or definite one-way design.

Because equal amounts of fabric are used for each color, I have not designated which fabric should be placed in what position. Rather, it is best to experiment before the initial "Tumbling Blocks" have been pieced, to decide on the layout you prefer. But to achieve the best optical effect, I recommend positioning the blocks in the same direction throughout the quilt.

Materials Needed

Fabric

Yardage amounts listed are what is needed for a quilt only. Refer to the yardage requirements for pillows, pillow shams, etc., as desired, and add accordingly.

Twin (90″ × 68″): 2¾ yards each of three fabrics
Full/queen (90″ × 86″): 3½ yards each of three fabrics
King (90″ × 102″): 4¼ yards each of three fabrics

Batting and Backing

Polyester fiberfill or wool or cotton batting large enough to complete your quilt.

A large, flat sheet or extra-wide fabric, large enough to use as a backing on your quilt. Three yards of

108″ sheeting (available at well-supplied fabric stores) will fit all sizes. Or you can use 44/45″-wide fabric as follows: For twin size, you need 5½ yards of 44/45″ wide fabric, cut into two pieces, each 2¾ yards long. Seam them together along the selvages (Fig. 6-1). For full/queen and king sizes, you need 8¼ yards of 44/45″ wide fabric, cut in three pieces, each 2¾ yards, seamed together along the selvages (Fig. 6-2).

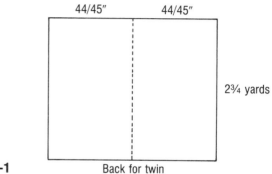

Fig. 6-1   Back for twin

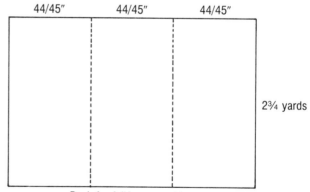

Fig. 6-2   Back for full/queen or king

When laying out the backing, batting, and quilt top, center the quilt top so the seams in the back are equal distances from the sides.

Don't Forget

Thread (for piecing your quilt face, as well as for hand or machine quilting, if desired)

String, yarn, or 1⁄16″ ribbon for tying your quilt, if you prefer

Graph paper or plain paper (which you have scored with 1″ squares) for pattern making

Making the Pattern

The Optika pattern requires only one pattern piece. For the bed-size quilts, you will need to make your own pattern piece using graph paper, gridded freezer paper, or tracing paper taped to a 1″ gridded cutting board. Graph paper is available in a variety of "squares-to-the-inch" sizes. It doesn't matter what size you choose, as long as the 1″ lines are clearly visible. If you are using smaller pieces of graph paper, carefully tape them together using clear tape, making sure the lines match up vertically and horizontally.

Here's how to draw your pattern piece: Start by marking a dot (Dot 1) on the corner of one square on the grid. (See the pattern guide on page 6-15). Now count 16½″ and mark Dot 2, as shown. Draw your solid line from Dot 1 to Dot 3 (11″), then draw your dashed line from Dot 3 to Dot 2 (5½″). Now draw a dashed line, 9½″, from Dot 2 to Dot 4. Draw a solid line across from Dot 4 to Dot 5 (11″). To complete your parallelogram, draw lines between Dots 1 and 5 and between Dots 3 and 4.

Note: Do not add seam allowances. Unlike in some quilt pattern books, the Optika patterns already include a ⅜″ seam allowance.

After you have drawn your pattern piece on the grid, double-check all measurements, and carefully cut it out (Fig. 6-3).

Fig. 6-3

Cutting the Fabric

This pattern is ideal for rotary cutting tools. Lay the fabric flat on a cutting surface, and fold it in half lengthwise, then in half again, also lengthwise. Lay the pattern piece as shown in Fig. 6-4, and carefully cut until you reach the end of the length of fabric. If done carefully, the cut edge of the first piece you cut can be used as a cut edge for the next piece, and so on. The number of pieces needed is given on the pattern guide on page 6-15.

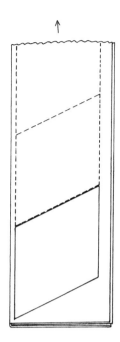

Fig. 6-4

Sewing the "Tumbling Blocks"

Hint #1: When one or both pattern pieces is being sewn on a bias (angle-cut) edge, it helps to pin the edges together to prevent pulling or stretching the fabric. Otherwise, it is not necessary to pin pieces together before sewing them. In fact, it's quicker and easier not to. Just be sure you're letting the machine do the work, and that you're not pulling, or "force-guiding," the fabric, which causes bias-cut fabrics to stretch or distort. You can also eliminate this potential problem by using a walking foot on your sewing machine.

Hint #2: Don't worry if your edges don't match perfectly when you are sewing them together. The seams are hidden inside the quilt. And the quilting stitches or ties help camouflage minor flaws. It's the total finished look that will make you proud to give or display your handiwork.

Hint #3: As you work, press all seam allowances toward the darker of the fabrics. This prevents seam allowances from being noticeable through lighter-colored fabrics.

1. After you have cut out all pieces, lay out one "Tumbling Block," consisting of three pieces (Fig. 6-5).

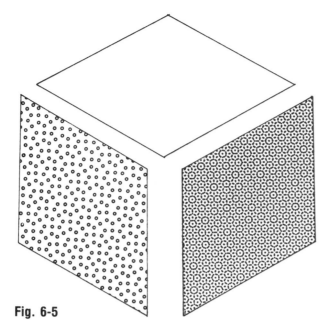

Fig. 6-5

2. Lay two of the three pieces right sides together and sew one seam, using a ⅜″ seam allowance. *The trick with this pattern is to start your seam about ⅜″ from the first angle and end the seam about ⅜″ before the edge of the fabric (Fig. 6-6).*

Fig. 6-6

3. Open the first two pieces, then lay the third piece of fabric, right sides together, on one of the other two. Lay them flat, with the extra one out of the way. Starting with the end away from what will be the center of the block, sew toward the center of the block, using a ⅜″ seam allowance and

leaving a ⅜″ space at the beginning and end of the seam (Fig. 6-7). Remember to back-tack the beginning and end of all seams.

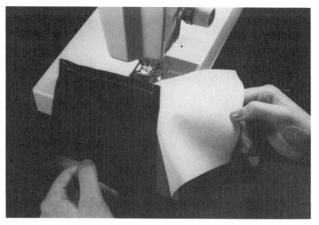

Fig. 6-7

4. Remove the block from your machine, and fold the entire piece in half, right sides together, so the remaining seam line is straight and even. (The first two seam lines will line up on top of each other.) Flatten the two pieces to be sewn, so that all seam allowances are pulled back and away from you. Starting at the end of where the first two seam lines meet, sew the remaining seam, again stopping about ⅜″ from the end (Fig. 6-8).

Fig. 6-8

5. Press all seam allowances toward the darker fabric, and you will have a block that lies perfectly flat (Fig. 6-9).

Fig. 6-9

6. Continue to do this with the remaining pieces. When you have completed all blocks, line them up in horizontal rows. You will need the following number of blocks and rows:

Twin—4 rows of 4 blocks
         3 rows of 5 blocks
Full/Queen—4 rows of 5 blocks
               3 rows of 6 blocks
King—4 rows of 6 blocks
         3 rows of 7 blocks

7. Sew the blocks together into horizontal rows. (Figure 6-10 shows the king size.) Every other row will be larger or smaller than the previous one. Again, leave a ⅜″ space at the beginning and ending of each seam.

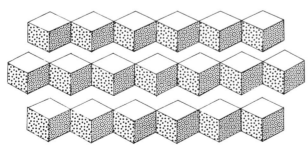

Fig. 6-10

8. Sew the rows together, as shown. Don't think of it as a long row of angles, but a series of little straight seams (Fig. 6-11). First lay the rows face up, so you can see where they will fit together.

Then fold one on top of the other, right sides together, taking only the first seam, and seaming it as though it were only two pieces of fabric. When you reach the corner, back-tack the seam, lift your machine needle and presser foot, and reposition the next seam to be sewn, pulling seam allowances back and away from you. The unsewn edges of the seam allowances will allow you to "flex" the fabric, without pulling or stretching it. Continue doing this to the end of the row. All vertical seams should match when the rows are put together. You can stretch a bias-cut edge on one of the pieces to ease it into place, if necessary.

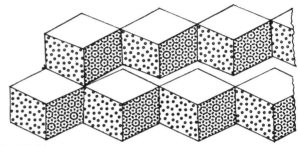

Fig. 6-11

9. You may have to go back and snip the corners of the seam allowance to allow the rows to lie flat, but, with practice, this won't even be necessary. Continue to sew the rows together until you have completed the face of your quilt (Fig. 6-12). Press all seams toward the darker fabric.

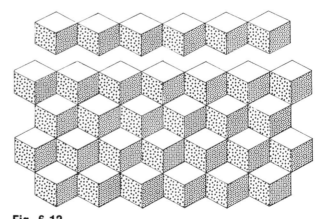

Fig. 6-12

10. The final step in completing your quilt face is to trim away all jagged edges (Fig. 6-13). After trimming the edges, your quilt face should measure approximately as follows:

Twin—92″ × 70″
Full/Queen—92″ × 88″
King—92″ × 104″

Fig. 6-13

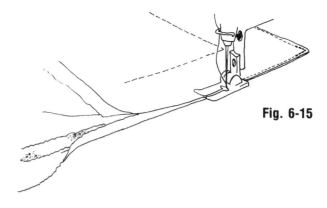

Fig. 6-15

Finishing the Quilt

1. Cut and seam the backing fabric, if necessary, to equal the size of your finished quilt top (see Figs. 6-1, 6-2).

2. Lay the backing (sheet, sheeting, or seamed fabric) right side down on a large, clean surface.

3. Place the polyester fiberfill or other batting on top of the backing.

4. Lay the quilt top right side up on the fiberfill. Hand baste, or pin using large safety pins, through all layers to hold them in place. (I prefer safety pins to straight pins because they save my hands and other body parts from pinpricks as I work.)

5. Using yarn, string, or 1/16″ ribbon, tie the layers firmly, or quilt the layers by hand or machine, as desired. Instructions follow.

6. Finish the edges, using bias tape or other decorative trim, as desired (Fig. 6-14). The edges can also be turned easily to the inside and sewn in place by machine (Fig. 6-15). You can insert piping, lace, or a ruffle at the edge with this method.

To Add Bias Tape

There are many ways to apply a bias taped edge, but in general, it is easiest if you sew a seam around your entire project, using a narrow seam allowance, to keep the layers from stretching or shifting *before* you apply the bias tape.

Starting in the middle of one side of your project, and using long straight pins, pin the bias tape around the entire piece, overlapping and folding under the last edge where it meets with your starting point. When you get to a corner, tuck the excess flatly and neatly inside of itself, by gently pushing it to one side with pointed scissors or a pin. It may help to open the bias tape so it is flat when you get to a corner, then pinch the excess to guide it into the fold at the corner (Fig. 6-16). Hand baste or topstitch by machine over the miter.

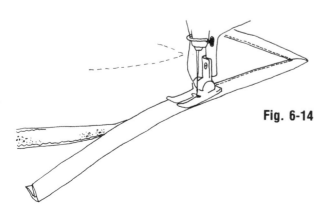

Fig. 6-14

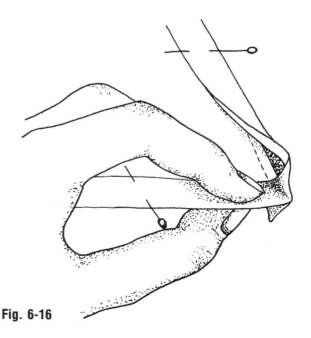

Fig. 6-16

To Tie Your Quilt

Tying your quilt is the easiest way to hold the layers together and provides a quick finish to your quilt. Baste or pin the layers of your quilt to hold them in place before starting to tie. It is not necessary to mark the points at which you will tie your quilt. Figure 6-17 shows where the ties should be placed.

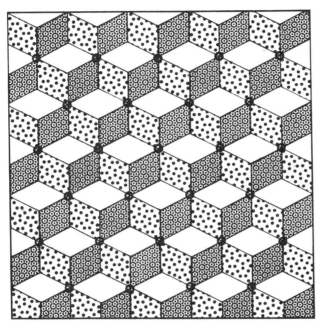

Fig. 6-17

Thread a large needle (one with a large eye, such as a tapestry needle) with yarn, $\frac{1}{16}''$ ribbon, or string (button or quilting thread also works well). Working from the top of the quilt, push the needle through all layers, drawing the thread through, but not all the way. Leave a 6″–8″ tail sticking out on top. About $\frac{1}{8}''$–$\frac{1}{4}''$ from the first stitch, draw the needle back up (from the back to the front) through all layers. Cut the thread, again leaving a tail about 6″–8″ long. Tie these two tails tightly together, using a double or triple knot to hold the tie securely in place. You can make a bow with the excess, or simply trim the tails to about 1″.

To Quilt by Machine

After the layers are securely pinned or basted, roll up one-half of the quilt tightly enough to allow it to fit under the head of your sewing machine. You can safety-pin it closed or use bicycle clips to hold the roll. With larger quilts, you may need a friend to help guide the bulk through while you are quilting the center block.

Starting with the seams shown in Fig. 6-18, stitch "anchoring" quilt lines to hold all layers in place. This stitching will secure all layers of fabric and help keep the remainder of the quilt from shifting. It also helps to smooth the top and bottom toward you occasionally, with one hand above and one hand below, palms pressed gently together, and fingers spread.

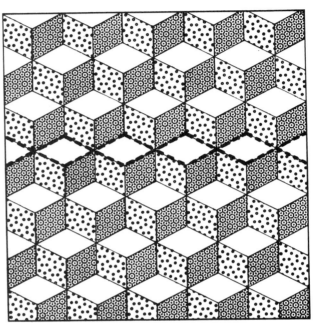

Fig. 6-18

After you have stitched the lines shown in Fig. 6-18, continue quilting by machine, following the outline of the pattern by sewing along the seam lines of the pieced quilt top. Be sure to back-tack the beginning and end of each quilting seam. It is easiest to quilt all horizontal rows first, in the same thread color, then change to a thread color that matches one of the diagonal rows to finish your quilt. When quilting along a seam that joins a solid color to a print fabric, try to keep your quilting stitches on the printed fabric, to the side of the seam.

Today's polyester fiberfills don't clump or shift as much as natural battings, like wool or cotton, because of the resins that hold the polyester fibers together. The stitching lines suggested here are adequate to hold polyester fiberfill in place, but you may wish to add some extra quilting lines or ties if you are using pure wool or cotton batting.

Alternate Method of Finishing

1. Another method of finishing your quilt is to sew the face to the backing, right sides together, leaving the top edge open. Because these seams are so long, it helps to pin the edges together before sewing, to hold them in place. Be sure the back is cut to the exact size of the face before sewing them together.

2. Before turning right side out, lay your top and backing, which have been sewn together on three sides, right side down on a large, clean, flat surface. If you don't have a large enough floor space, lay it on as large a table as you can, with the open, unseamed end hanging over the edge of the table, and the bottom half of the quilt lying flat on the table. Place the polyester fiberfill on top and trim it to the exact size of the quilt.

3. Starting at the end opposite the opening, roll the entire quilt, like a sleeping bag, or jelly roll, until you have a long "tube" of fabric and batting.

4. Carefully reach inside the layers of fabric (between the face and backing), and slowly pull the tube inside-out, through the opening.

5. Slowly unwrap the quilt, which will open, filled with fiberfill, and with three of the edges finished. (Practice with a sock. First, roll the sock, starting at the toe, and pull the cuff back over the roll. Slowly unroll it from the inside out, reaching inside the sock, between the layers, and pulling gently on the roll.)

6. Lay the quilt on a large, flat surface, and pin or baste through all layers. Hand or machine quilt, or tie it, as described above.

7. Turn the remaining edges to the inside, pin to hold, and machine stitch to close.

Make a Crib Quilt or Wall Hanging (50″ × 40″)

Materials Needed

Face: 1¼ yards each of three fabrics

Backing: 1¾ yards of 44/45″ wide fabric

Polyester fiberfill to 54″ × 44″

Thread (for piecing your quilt face, as well as for hand or machine quilting, if desired)

String, yarn, or 1/16″ ribbon for tying your quilt, if you prefer

Graph paper or plain paper (which you have scored with 1″ squares) for pattern making

1. See "Getting Started" in the instructions for the large quilts. For this size quilt you can trace your pattern piece directly from the template on page 6-16. **Do not add seam allowances.** Cut out the pattern, then cut 44 pieces of each of three fabrics. Be sure to use your rotary cutting tools to cut several layers of fabric at the same time.

2. Follow Steps 1 through 5 in the piecing instructions for completing the "Tumbling Blocks," page 6-4. Continue until you have pieced 44 blocks.

3. Sew the blocks into four horizontal rows of five blocks and four rows of six blocks (see Steps 7, 8, and 9, page 6-6). Starting with a row of six blocks, and alternating the rows, sew them together as described for the large quilts.

4. Trim the finished piece to a rectangle approximately 50″ × 40″.

5. Refer to "Finishing the Quilt" in the instructions for the large quilts to complete the crib quilt or wall hanging. (This pattern is simply a miniature version of the large quilt.)

You will probably want to make loops of fabric to sew to the top of your finished wall hanging project or just behind the upper edge (hidden) to allow for a dowel rod to hang it.

To Make the Loops

For **hidden loops**, cut three pieces of fabric 1½″ × 4″. Fold the long edges inward to meet at the center, then fold the whole strip in half lengthwise. Using a straight stitch, sew through all layers along the "open" edge to make a small "ribbon" of fabric. Attach one in the middle of the upper edge of the wall hanging, and the remaining two at either side on the upper edge. Tack these to the wall hanging through all layers using your sewing machine, or hand sew them in place.

For **decorative loops**, cut three pieces of matching fabric 3″ × 5″. Fold these in half, right sides together, to create 1½″ × 5″ pieces. Using a ⅜″ seam allowance, sew a straight line down the 5″ raw edge. Turn these tubes right side out and press so the seam is centered on one side. Fold these in half widthwise to hide the seam. Attach to the top of your wall hanging by machine, spacing the loops evenly (Fig. 6-19).

Fig. 6-19

For **bow loops**, cut three pieces of wide ribbon, each 24″ long. Fold these in half and tack them to the top edge of your wall hanging by hand or machine, evenly spaced. Tie these loosely around a decorative pole or dowel rod.

This project finishes to a perfect size for use as a table topper, lap quilt, or sofa throw.

Make a 16″ Throw Pillow

Fabric Requirements

Face: Use leftover scrap from quilt or ¼ yard each of three fabrics

Back: ½ yard of a matching fabric

Ruffle or cord (if desired): ⅝ yard

1. Trace the pillow pattern piece from page 6-16 onto tracing paper. **Do not add seam allowances.** Cut out the pattern, then cut 14 pieces of each of three fabrics.

2. Follow Steps 1 through 5 in the piecing instructions for completing the "Tumbling Blocks," page 6-4. Continue until 14 blocks are pieced.

3. Sew the blocks into two rows of four blocks and two rows of three. Alternate the rows and sew them together. (See Steps 7, 8, and 9, page 6-6).

4. Cut this finished piece into a square approximately 17″ square.

5. You may wish to first quilt the pillow face by layering it with a plain muslin backing and fiberfill, cut to the same size as the face, then hand or machine quilt along the seams. This is not necessary, simply a matter of preference.

6. See the instructions for making and applying ruffling and bias cording, page 6-13. With raw edges together, and with a ⅜″ seam allowance, sew bias cording (Fig. 6-20) or a ruffle (Fig. 6-21) around the entire pillow face. You will need about 2 yards of bias cording or finished ruffling to go around the pillow. For a knife-edge pillow, with no extra trim, you can eliminate this step.

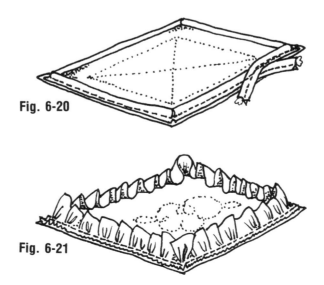

Fig. 6-20

Fig. 6-21

7. Cut two pieces of a backing fabric, 10″ × 17″. Finish one 17″ edge on each of these two pieces with a double-folded hem, machine stitched.

8. Lay the pillow right side up, with ruffle or cording toward the center. Place the backing right side down, on the pillow, overlapping the finished edges evenly in the center. Pin around the edges (Fig. 6-22).

9. Sew around the entire pillow, following the seam used to sew the cording or ruffle in place, or using a ⅜″ seam allowance. Turn inside out

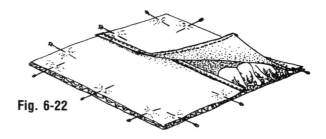

Fig. 6-22

through the overlapped backing. Trim away any excess around the seams before turning.

10. Insert a 15″ or 16″ pillow form.

Make Your Own 15″–16″ Pillow Form

1. Save your scrap fiberfill.

2. Cut two 18″ squares of any white or ivory fabric.

3. Sew these together on three sides, using a ½″ seam allowance. Turn right side out.

4. Cut two 17″ squares of leftover fiberfill, and carefully slide them into the pillow cover. Con-

tinue to stuff smaller bits of fiberfill between the squares, until the pillow is plump, but not too hard.

5. To finish, whipstitch the opening by hand. I call this a 15″–16″ finished size because the finished size will vary according to the plumpness of the pillow.

Make a Removable Chair Pad Cover

Note: An additional ⅓ yard of one of the fabrics is required for each chair pad.

1. Complete the 16″ pillow cover as explained above in "Make a 16″ Throw Pillow."

2. Cut two strips of fabric, 44″ × 5″. With a roll-hem attachment for your sewing machine, or a narrow double fold, hem around all sides of both strips. You may wish to fold one corner of each end to the inside and machine stitch to hold in place, to create pointed ends. Fold each strip in half, matching the two short ends, to create two tie ends, and pinch or pleat at the fold to gather. At what will be the back two corners, machine stitch the ties to the pillow cover, on the underside of the finished pillow, under the ruffle (Fig. 6-23).

3. To make a removable chair pad insert, purchase or make a 15″–16″ pillow form. With a long needle and double heavy-duty thread, run the

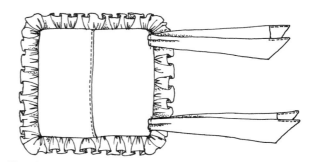

Fig. 6-23

thread through the center of the pillow form, leaving a "tail" of thread about 6″ long. Bring the needle back through about ½″ from the first stitch, and tie the ends of the thread, pulling tightly to form a "tuft" in the center.

Two matching chair pads with inserts make a lovely rocker set.

Make a Standard Pillow Sham

Fabric Requirements

Face: Use leftover scrap from quilt or ½ yard each of three fabrics

Back: ⅔ yard

Ruffle (if desired): ⅞ yard

1. See "Getting Started" in the instructions for the large quilts. Trace the pillow sham pattern piece from page 6-16 onto tracing paper. **Do not add seam allowances.** Cut out the pattern, then cut 13 pieces of each of two fabrics, and 18 pieces of the third fabric.

2. Follow Steps 1 through 5 in the piecing instructions for completing the "Tumbling Blocks," page 6-4. Continue until you have pieced 13 blocks.

3. Sew the blocks into two rows of four blocks and one row of five. Place the row of five blocks between the rows of four and sew these rows together as described in Steps 7, 8, and 9, page 6-6. Add the remaining five pieces as shown (Fig. 6-24).

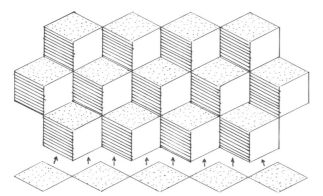

Fig. 6-24

4. Cut this finished piece into a rectangle approximately 22″ × 28″.

5. You may wish to first quilt the sham face by layering it with a plain muslin backing and fiberfill, cut to the same size as the face, then hand or machine quilt along the seams. This is not necessary, simply a matter of preference.

6. See the instructions for making and applying ruffling and bias cording on page 6-13. With raw edges together, sew bias cording or a ruffle around the entire sham face (see Figs. 6-20, 6-21). You will need about 3 yards of bias cording or finished ruffling to go around the pillow sham. This is sewn to the right side of the pillow sham. For a knife-edge pillow sham, with no extra trim, you can eliminate this step.

7. Cut two pieces of a backing fabric, 16″ × 24″, finishing one 24″ edge on each piece with a narrow double-folded hem, machine stitched.

8. Lay the pillow sham right side up, with ruffle or cording pressed toward the center. Place the backing right side down, on the sham, overlapping the finished edges evenly in the center. Pin around the edges (see Fig. 6-22).

9. Sew around the entire pillow sham, following the seam used to sew the ruffling and/or cording in place Turn inside out through the overlapped backing. Trim away any excess around the seams before turning right side out (Fig. 6-25).

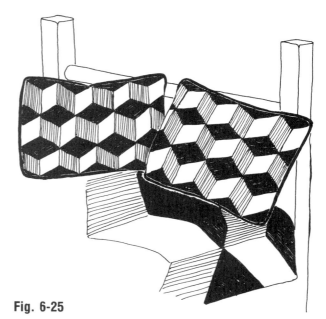

Fig. 6-25

How to Make Matching Ruffling and Bias Cording for Pillows, Shams, and Chair Pads

Ruffling

You will need about ⅝ yard of extra fabric for ruffles around pillows and chair pads. You will need about ⅞ yard for pillow shams.

1. From the width of the fabric (44/45″) cut three 7″ strips (four strips for pillow shams), and sew them together on the short ends to make a long circle of fabric. Press the seam allowances open (Fig. 6-26).

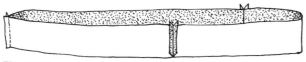

Fig. 6-26

2. Fold the circle in half lengthwise, so the raw edges meet, and right sides face out. Press.

3. With a wide basting stitch, sew about ¼″ from the raw edge (Fig. 6-27).

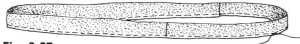

Fig. 6-27

4. Divide the circle equally into quarters, identifying the quarter marks with a straight pin. Pin the circle to the center of each straight edge on all four sides of your project, using the pins that mark the quarters to hold the ruffle in place.

5. Pull the basting stitch until the circle gathers evenly into a ruffle equal to the size of the project you are working on. Use straight pins to hold the ruffle in place around the outer edge of the project, raw edges together, as you gather it to fit.

Bias Cording

You will need ⅝ yard of matching fabric to make your own bias cording.

1. Cut a 1½″-wide strip of fabric on the bias. The strip of bias-cut fabric should be several inches longer than the measurement around the edge of the project you wish to trim.

2. Using purchased cording, wrap the bias strip around the cording so that wrong sides and raw edges meet. With a zipper foot attachment, stitch close to the cord, but not too snug, through both layers of fabric (Fig. 6-28).

3. The simplest application of the finished bias cording is to begin sewing it on one straight edge, keeping the raw edges of the bias tape and your project even, but with the starting end angled off the edge. Sew around the entire project, clipping the seam allowance of the bias tape at the corners. When you reach your starting point, overlap the bias tape, sewing over the angled end, and carefully angle the final end to sew it off the edge (see Fig. 6-20). Clip it to trim.

You may also apply bias tape by starting in the middle of one side, but start your seam about 2″ from the end of the bias tape. Sew all around as described above, but when you get to where you started, open the seam on the 2″ tail of the bias tape and pull back the fabric to show the cord. Clip off the 2″ of cord, and fold the fabric that is left in half, to create a 1″ tail (fold the fabric to the inside, so that only the right side shows). Cut the other end of the bias tape so it ends exactly where the first cord now starts. Wrap the folded bias tape fabric around this raw edge, and finish your seam.

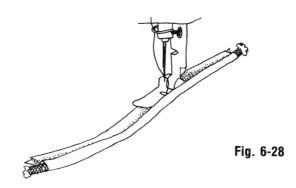

Fig. 6-28

Make a Placemat

Fabric Requirements

Face: Use leftover scrap from quilt or ¼ yard each of three fabrics

Back: ½ yard of fabric will allow enough for *two* placemats

1. Trace the pillow pattern piece from page 6-16 onto tracing paper. Cut out the pattern, then cut 16 of each of your three fabrics.

2. Follow Steps 1 through 5 in the piecing instructions for completing the "Tumbling Blocks," page 6-4. Continue until 16 blocks are pieced.

3. Sew the blocks into four rows of four blocks. Sew these rows together as described in Steps 7, 8, and 9, page 6-6.

4. Cut this finished piece into a rectangle approximately 17″ × 20″ (Fig. 6-29).

5. Cut a rectangle of backing fabric 17″ × 20″. Place the back and the pieced face right sides together. Sew together with a ⅜″ seam allowance all around, except for a 4″ opening centered on one of the seams. Clip the corners and turn inside out

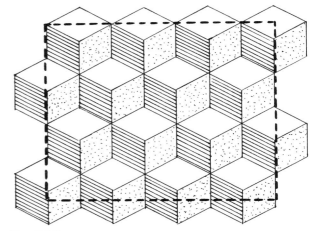

Fig. 6-29

through the opening. Hand or machine stitch the opening and press all around.

6. To minimize raveling or fraying of the seams on the inside when these are washed, you may wish to "quilt" along the seam lines, even though these do not have fiberfill. (You may add fiberfill, if you wish.)

Optika Pattern Guide for Twin, Full/Queen, and King Quilts

Dimensions include ⅜″ seam allowance.

Cut the following number of pieces of each of your three fabrics:

For twin size, cut 31 pieces of each color.
For full/queen size, cut 38 pieces of each color.
For king size, cut 45 pieces of each color.

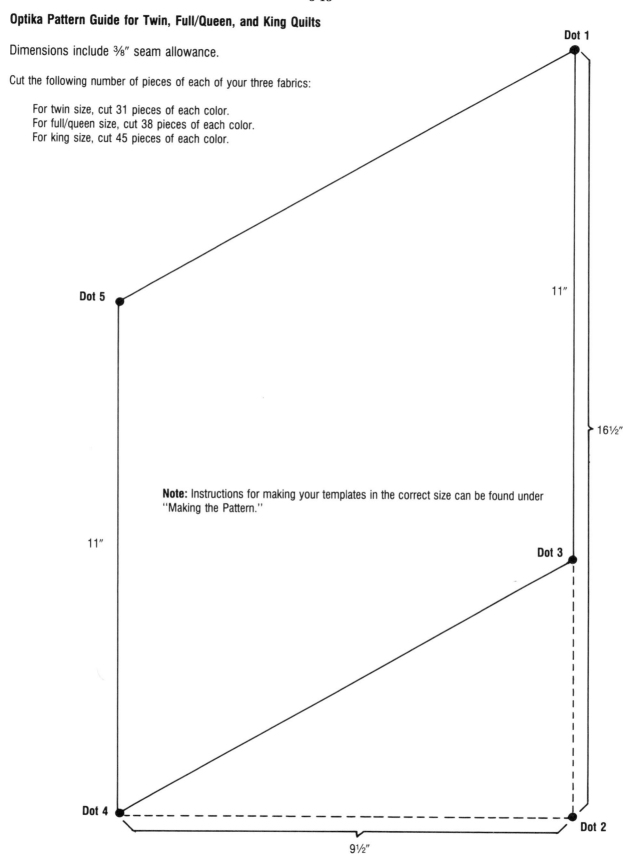

Dot 1

Dot 5

11″

16½″

Note: Instructions for making your templates in the correct size can be found under "Making the Pattern."

11″

Dot 3

Dot 4

Dot 2

9½″

Optika Templates

For the crib quilt/wall hanging, and the pillow sham, use the larger template given here. For the crib quilt and wall hanging, cut 44 pieces of each of three fabrics. For the pillow sham, cut 13 pieces of each of two fabrics and 18 pieces of the third fabric.

For the 16″ pillow, the chair pad, and the placemat, use the smaller template given here. For the pillow and chair pad, cut 14 pieces each of three fabrics. For the placemat, cut 16 pieces each of three fabrics.

INDEX